My editor had ok'd the story, "The Unveiling of a Quack," and now I faced the man whom the power of the press would squash like a bug.

"Five times," he said quietly in response to my question, "the Medical Society of the County of New York sent a committee here to investigate my methods. I let them see patients, X-rays, records, everything."

"And what were the results of those investigations?"

"I do not know," Dr. Max Gerson replied. "They have never revealed them."

I left Dr. Gerson and wrote the Medical Society of the County of New York, as follows: "We have no feelings one way or the other concerning Dr. Gerson's treatment except that of public responsibility . . . Is there any way we can be advised of the nature of your findings?"

Their reply was to embark me on the strangest, most frustrating story of my life . . . the *story of a man who by absolute record had cured people of cancer, including children, and his incredibly courageous and lonely fight against the forces of organized medicine.*

"I agree with you that Dr. Gerson's cancer therapy had great merits and know with which difficulties Dr. Gerson had to struggle. I would be grateful to you if you try to tell the people of America about Dr. Gerson's merits and about the results he obtained with his therapy . . . I wish you the best in your difficult task."

— Dr. Albert Schweitzer

HAS Dr. MAX GERSON A TRUE CANCER CURE?

BY S.J. HAUGHT

MAJOR BOOKS • CANOGA PARK, CALIFORNIA

"Stay close to nature,
and its eternal laws will protect you."
—Dr. Gerson, to his daughter

This paperback published by

MAJOR BOOKS
21335 Roscoe Boulevard
Canoga Park, California 91304

Major Books
    First Printing . . . . . . September 1976
    Second Printing . . . . March 1977
    Third Printing . . . . June 1978
    Fourth Printing . . . . . November 1979
    All Rights Reserved.

Printed by arrangement with London Press
North Hollywood, California

ISBN 0-89041-272-3

Library of Congress Catalog Card Number
76-12707

PRINTED IN THE UNITED STATES OF AMERICA

CHAPTER ONE

A change in the weather seems to have a strange effect on some people. I don't suppose I was the first reporter to have noticed it, but let the weather turn suddenly warm and you can expect a rash of letters and phone calls from readers who want to air their grievances or complain about some personal persecution. Newspapers often refer to these folks as the "lunatic fringe."

But more than once among those relaters of incredible stories I have found a genuine case of injustice. A newspaper, I felt, should be the last hope and refuge for bewildered souls who have been buffeted and torn by a world that can be harsh and cynical, who have been elbowed out of the way by insolent officials and exploited by unscrupulous schemers, and who don't know where else to turn. A newspaper should be more than comic strips and puzzles; it should be the conscience of society.

Today the sun was shining. After weeks of bitter cold and slush, New York had turned unseasonably warm. Topcoats disappeared from the streets and office workers crossed Third Avenue in their shirts to pick up containers of coffee from the little delicatessens.

A number of letters awaited me at my desk that morning — a note of thanks from a singer I'd written a feature story about; a letter from a woman in upstate New York who wanted more information on a plastic surgeon I'd written about, and a three-page typewritten letter that began: "To Whom it May Concern:"

"My name is — —, I'm 28 years old and a mother of a seven-year-old daughter. I'm writing my story in hope that it will help others and to help me receive financial aid. On May 28th, 1957, I was operated on at

5

— — Hospital for a blood-vessel tumor located in the abdomen. It was the size of a grapefruit and extended into both hips. Five days later they started me on deep X-ray therapy. Three weeks later the tumor was back again. Then three months later, even though I had been receiving deep therapy consisting of 47 treatments at 15 minutes each, the tumor was as large as it had been before the operation. I'd like to add that these treatments had left me badly burned across the stomach and the lower part of the back. Now this operation and all these X-ray treatments did me absolutely no good, and left me $1,100 in debt, as I was just as bad as I had been in the beginning.

"The doctors that I had gave me only from two to six months to live starting from the time of the operation, which, however, I did not know at this time. After the 47 treatments, I was given a month off from therapy. It was at this time that Mrs. — —, a friend of mine, told me about her mother who had lymphosarcoma and went to Dr. Gerson three years ago. She is completely cured now.

"On Sept. 18, 1957, I went to see Dr. — — for my checkup and suspecting that I had cancer, since I had all the symptoms, I asked him directly if it was. He told me 'Oh, don't be silly.' Then I asked him if there was anything besides therapy that I could use and he replied 'No, there was only therapy and I had to have it for a long time.'

"On Sept. 19, 1957, I went to see Dr. Max Gerson of Park Avenue, New York City. He examined me and informed me that the tumor was back and was a large mass and that I definitely did have cancer. He admitted me to his 'Oakland Manor Cancer Clinic' in Nanuet, New York, on Sept. 23, 1957. He has discovered the cause of cancer as well as the cure, the cure being a corrective diet along with certain medications. Five days after I was on the diet at his clinic, as God is my witness, the tumor shrank to the size of a golf ball and two months later had completely disappeared. Even though these X-ray treatments left me approximately 90% sterile at that time, Dr. Gerson says that in two years time I can have a completely normal child. Everything Dr. Gerson told me would happen did come true, so that I'm certain that what he said about my being able to have children will come true, too, because I have already noticed signs of my reproductive organs returning to normal.

"I have been on this diet for five months now and I'm feeling fine and getting stronger every day, without the aid of any drugs. I am doing light housework, my own cooking, and the laundry for my husband and myself. I also have my daughter home on weekends. During the week she lives with my mother. I go to Dr. Gerson every month for a checkup and according to the physical examination and metabolism test I'm improving rapidly.

"The diet consists of: orange juice, greenjuice, liver juice and carrot juice. I take 12 glasses of juice every day made with a special grinder and press. I receive a B-12 shot with liver extract twice a week, and two coffee enemas a day. My meals consist of fresh fruit, cottage cheese, skim milk, and yogurt. My diet costs over $50 a week . . .

"My husband's income at the present time is $56 a week, take-home pay. My family has helped me as much as they can. Now that they can no longer help, it is impossible for us to make ends meet on $56 a week, since we have rent, gas, electric, oil, phone, car insurance and life insurance on my husband and daughter to pay also. I have asked for help from the Cancer Society and the Public Welfare, but because the Medical Society refuses to recognize Dr. Gerson's method of treatment, these agencies refuse to give me financial aid. The Public Welfare did give me one emergency check to pay some overdue bills.

"Mrs. — —, my case worker, informed me that my case is before the medical board and that I can no longer receive funds until the board approves of this treament. Despite the fact that Dr. Gerson has sent them two letters about my condition up to the present time, they still refuse me any further aid. Why they are having such a hard time accepting this doctor and his treatment I can't understand, since he is a genuine medical doctor. He is known in Europe and England for his work. His book *A Cancer Therapy* is due out this month . . .

"Dr. Gerson said that, altogether, I would have to be on this diet 1½ years to be completely cured. He considers a person completely cured when the liver is normal and the blood purified and the body rebuilt. Therefore, if I went off this diet now due to the lack of funds, it would mean certain death since the tumor would come back and this type kills quickly.

"I hope and pray that those of you that are reading this letter will know of someone or some agency that can give me financial aid until the year and a half is up. I also hope that by writing this letter, I can save some other person or persons from going through the mental and physical torture that only a cancer patient can know.

"Dr. Gerson is only interested in helping mankind and I hope and pray that some day he will be recognized for his work with cancer."

My first impulse was to drop this letter in the wastebasket and get on with my work. As though a diet could cure cancer! And if this Dr. Gerson — whoever he was — had "discovered the cause of cancer as well as the cure," his name would certainly be on everybody's lips as one of the great saviors of mankind. Instead, I'd never heard of him.

But the letter did ring of sincerity. Besides, I can never throw away typewritten pages. As a writer, I can too easily visualize an editor disdainfully tossing aside one of my manuscripts without realizing the labor that went into it. So I stuck the letter in my top drawer and went on with something else.

But everytime I opened that drawer to get a pencil or to get a manuscript for re-write, my eye fell on those five pleading words: "To Whom It May Concern." It was like a voice crying in the wilderness. And somehow it seemed criminal to shut up that voice within a desk drawer, to turn my back on it without first ascertaining whether my help was truly needed.

So one day I re-read the letter. Once again I was conscious of the fact that in her own mind at least, the writer was desperately in need of help. If she was being taken advantage of by one of those cancer quacks I'd read so much about, wouldn't that in itself make a story? Wouldn't I be performing a public service by exposing the man?

I took the letter to my editor's office and explained what I had in mind. He agreed it was worth a "check-out" and told me to go ahead with it. Sometimes you don't get the story you go after; you get an entirely different one.

I went back to my desk and reached for the phone. I didn't know it then, but I was embarking on the strangest story of my life!

CHAPTER TWO

My sympathies were all with the woman who had written me the letter. From the television exposes I had seen and from numerous articles I had read on this very subject, I was sure she had fallen into the hands of that vilest of all men, the cancer quack, and that she was being bled for every last penny she had.

My first move, since Dr. Gerson was an M.D., was to write to the American Medical Association and ask them what they thought of his cancer treatment. They replied that they did not engage in the approval or disapproval of treatments.

"According to our biographic records," they said, "Dr. Gerson was graduated from Albert-Ludwigs Universitat Medizinsche Fakultat, Freiburg, Baden, Germany, in 1909, and was licensed to practice medicine in New York in 1938. We have been informed that he has been suspended from membership in his local medical society for a period of two years, beginning March 4, 1958. The specific charge was his use of a radio interview to discuss his work in the treatment of cancer.

"We have had record of Dr. Gerson and his diet treatment for various diseases for a considerable period of time. We commented on Dr. Gerson, and his reluctance to reveal the details of his treatment, in an editorial in *The Journal* for Nov. 16, 1946. We are sorry we do not have tear sheets or reprints available. Therein it was pointed out that although Dr. Gerson had been requested to do so, he had failed or refused to acquaint the medical profession with the details of his treatment.

"For a time after that, Dr. Gerson was employed by an organization calling itself the Madison Foundation for Biochemical Research, Inc., of New York. The

Foundation, however, advised this Association that a report had been made during the years 1948 and 1949 of the findings observed in cases of cancer in which the Gerson dietary treatment was used. It was stated: 'The Medical Advisory Board finds that insufficient evidence has been presented to warrant any claim that the Gerson dietary treatment is a cure for cancer . . .'

"Your reference to 'who judges which man is a quack — and how?' is answered, we believe, in the enclosed leaflet entitled 'Mechanical Quackery'."

I gathered from the tone of this letter that the AMA couldn't come right out and say that Dr. Gerson was a quack, but they could let the facts speak for themselves. And in this case, the facts spoke volumes.

I had no doubt that the AMA had handed me a weapon of considerable potency to use in my investigation. Unconsciously, perhaps, I was glad that they had so quickly and conveniently prepared a road for me. It's human nature to prefer the smooth, the even, and the direct way. No one likes to go chasing down a hundred byways and back roads searching for what may be only an illusion of truth.

But there are little things — seemingly insignificant at first — that grow into monsters when you look closely at them.

Two phrases in the AMA letter, ostensibly unrelated, caught my attention: ". . . use of a radio interview to discuss his work in the treatment of cancer" and " . . . failed or refused to acquaint the medical profession with the details of his treatment."

Why, I wondered, would a doctor neglect to acquaint the medical profession with the details of his treatment and at the same time appear on a radio program to discuss them? If he had something to hide, if he was a quack, I could understand his reluctance to reveal his methods. But on the other hand, why would he place himself in jeopardy on a radio program?

A legitimate question? I decided to find out.

In answer to my query about Dr. Gerson, the American Cancer Society sent me a printed resume. Apparently they had received inquiries before.

Dated July, 8, 1957, the statement read:

"Dr. Max Gerson came to this country from Austria in the early 1940s. His work in the 'treatment' of cancer by dietary methods had previously been used in Austria for the management of both cancer and tuberculosis. From 1946 to 1950 he used this treatment at the Gotham Hospital in New York City until, during the later year, his affiliation with that hospital was terminated. At present he treats patients in his own nursing home outside the city. He also maintains an office at 815 Park Avenue. Although, to our knowledge, Dr. Gerson has never been indicted or expelled from any medical society, it is our understanding that he is at present under surveillance by the Licensing Board of New York State and that his malpractice insurance has been discontinued.

"Dr. Gerson's proposed method of treatment and the method of treatment that he is using in his sanitorium near New York City is essentially that of diet. The principal ingredients being stressed are liver, vitamins and fresh vegetables, with emphasis on cabbage. The food is not to be prepared in aluminum utensils, and glass utensils are preferred. The vegetables are chopped up and made into a juice by means of special chopping and juicing machines which are offered to his patients for sale at around $150. Frequent and copious enemas are also used as a feature in the treatment. Patients are usually treated as inpatients at the sanitorium and allowed to return to their homes under treatment after Dr. Gerson thinks their condition permits their so doing. They are taught to give their own injections of liver at home and he has advocated that the treatment be continued for a period of one year. As you undoubtedly know, there is no evidence at the present time that any food or any combination of foods specifically affects the course of any cancer in man.

"In 1947 a Committee of the New York County Medical Society reviewed Dr. Gerson's work thoroughly, including the study of histories of patients who were said to have benefited by the treatment. This study failed to disclose any scientific evidence of objective improvement in patients which could be attributed to the treatment of Dr. Gerson. I should like to refer you to the report of the Council on Pharmacy and Chemistry of the American Medical Association appearing in the *Journal of the American Medical Association,* January 8, 1949, a part of which is concerned with Gerson's work.

"Dr. Gerson received a good deal of publicity five or six years ago when the son of John Gunther, suffering from recurrent brain tumor, underwent the treatment. Pressure symptoms were apparently temporarily relieved, but the brief remission has been attributed, by competent authorities, to dehydration. Another young boy in whom we were interested was brought to Gerson by his parents after an amputation had been advised for a bone tumor. Following a prolonged stay at the Gerson place, the youngster was returned home in a pitiable state of malnutrition.

"The American Cancer Society can find no acceptable evidence that the treatment proposed by Dr. Max Gerson produces any objective benefit in the treatment of cancer."

Well, they ought to know, I thought. A few more pieces of such information would provide me with the basis for an expose on cancer quacks, how they deceive the public, and cause untold harm by preying on the ignorance of cancer sufferers.

I found the report referred to by the American Cancer Society and read:

"Another 'treatment' for cancer involving dietary restrictions is that of Dr. Max B. Gerson of New York City, who has been reported by the *Journal* to be using a dietary and salt-controlled method that is said to be supported by a Robinson Foundation for cancer research located at 14 Wall Street, New York. The *Journal* pointed out that Gerson had been previously connected with a diet method falsely proposed as an advance in the treatment of tuberculosis and that the research 'foundation' for cancer was actually financed by two business enterprises.

"The diet was said to make the body highly hypersensitive, so that ordinary anesthesia might be fatal, a conjecture that is wholly unfounded and apparently designed to appeal to the cancer victim already fearful of a surgical operation, which might offer the only effective means for eradication of the disease. However, there is no scientific evidence whatsoever to indicate that modifications in the dietary intake of food or other nutritional essentials are of any specific value in the control of cancer."

Next I sought out the Nov. 16, 1946, edition of the *Journal of the American Medical Association* to read the editorial they'd mentioned. It was the "Kiss of Death" for Dr. Gerson.

"Some years ago a technique called the Gerson-Sauerbruch-Hermannsdorfer diet was claimed to be a notable advance in the treatment of tuberculosis. Gerson proposed, by the use of these diets, to change the nature of the soil in which the tubercle bacillus lives. According to the reports, Gerson had discovered accidentally some improvement in a patient with lupus who was on a salt-free diet. The good results in many types of tuberculosis reported by Gerson were apparently not susceptible of duplication by most other observers . . .

"For several years now the *Journal* has been receiving requests from people all over the United States for information about Dr. Max Gerson, who is said to be using a dietary and salt-controlled method for treating cancer patients at the Gotham Hospital in New York. The *Journal* has on several occasions requested Dr. Gerson to supply information as to the details of his method of treatment but has thus far received no satisfactory reply. A preliminary report, 'Dietary Considerations in Malignant Neoplastic Diseases,' appeared in the *Review of Gastroenterology*, November-December 1945, page 419.

"In the meantime occasional references have appeared in the press to the Robinson Foundation for cancer research, located at 14 Wall Street, New York, which is said to be supporting the Gerson method. In the last session of Congress, hearings were held on a bill to appropriate $100,000,000 of federal money for research on cancer. Dr. Gerson is said to have presented five of his patients to these public hearings. Fortunately for the American people this presentation received little, if any, newspaper publicity. However, Raymond Swing, radio commentator, in a broadcast over A.B.C. July 3, 1946, told the world that the Gerson cancer treatment was producing remarkable results. People who sent for a copy of the broadcast were referred to Dr. George Miley at the Gotham Hospital.

"Now there has come to hand through a prospective patient of Dr. Max Gerson a schedule of diets alleged to be beneficial in such cases. The patient was a man aged 83, with cancer of the stomach and multiple metastases, whom Dr. Gerson had never seen. Nevertheless he provided a complete diet for a period of four weeks, given in minute detail. The diet, which resembles that given in the *Review of Gastroenterology*, forbade tobacco, spices, coffee, tea, chocolate, alcohol, white sugar, white flour, pastries, and sausages; in short no canned, preserved, sulfured, frozen, smoked, salted, refined, or bottled food. It specified that there must be no salt, soda, sodium bicarbonate, fats, or oil. It forbade also, for sometime, the use of meat, fish, eggs, milk butter, cheese, and bread. It permitted fruit but nothing from cans. It specified a mixed fresh apple and carrot juice and other fruit juices and vegetables all freshly prepared and saltless. It forbade the use of pressure cookers. Basis of the diet was a special soup, of which the unfortunate victim is supposed to take 1 quart a day. The formula included a large parsley root, 3 or 4 leeks, 1 large celery knob, 4 or 5 tomatoes, 3 to 5 large potatoes, 2 or 3 large onions and 3 to 5 carrots. Also permitted was some oatmeal. The medication included Lugo's solution daily, niacin in large amounts daily, liver powder with iron daily, lubile — dried bile salts — one capsule four times a day, brewers' yeast three times daily, dicalcium phosphate with viosterol one tablet eight times a day, phosphorous compound 1 teaspoon dissolved in each glass of juice, 3 cc. of crude liver extract intramuscularly several times a week and also some injected vitamin K. The formula says that there should be no other medication because it can be harmful and dangerous, and it warns particularly against the use of anesthesia, because it says that the body becomes highly hypersensitive through this diet and that the usual anesthesia might become fatal. As part of the routine, Dr. Gerson insists that a patient have at least one copious bowel movement a day, preferably two, and he has provided a formula for an enema to secure this activity . . ."

It took no great imagination to draw the conclusion

that the medical profession looked with disfavor upon Dr. Gerson. But what worried me most was that a man like this should be allowed to continue his practice. How would the average person, stricken with cancer, know that this M.D. was a charlatan? Suppose they should go to him in good faith, believing that they would receive the same treatment from him as from any other doctor? When your very life is at stake, wouldn't it be important to know?

Apparently no such protection existed. The American citizen and taxpayer, confused with dread and anguish in the darkest moment of his life, might easily stumble into the clutches of a quack and forfeit his life. Sad to say, the old principle of *caveat emptor* — let the buyer beware — seemed to obtain here. There was no Better Business Bureau to protect him.

I had the time to investigate, and even if nobody had actually come right out and called Dr. Gerson a quack, the letters and articles had been suffused with a heavy sarcasm which served the purpose of putting him in a ridiculous light. It was warning enough to any person with time enough to seek it out.

But time is one commodity cancer sufferers cannot spare. They suspect they have only a little of it left, and they are disinclined to expend it checking into the background of a doctor — especially if he comes highly recommended by a friend.

Dismayed by this state of affairs, I wrote to the Medical Society of the County of New York, asking if they would approve or disapprove of Dr. Gerson's cancer treatment.

Their answer: "It is not within the province of the Medical Society of the County of New York to pass upon the efficacy or adequacy of any doctor's treatment of his own patients.

"Doctor Gerson is a member of this Society but is presently under suspension from the rights and privileges of membership, as a result of personal publicity."

There it was again, the reluctance to condemn but the willingness to add a "dig" on the end, as though a businessman, asked about his partner's character, should say, "Oh, John is all right, I guess, if he can just stay away from that liquor!"

But there were, undoubtedly, many things I did not know about the medical fraternity. There were, perhaps, certain ground rules to observe. There was the matter of ethics. Still, the cancer sufferer cannot be concerned with those. He needs — he must have — protection.

More pressing than my story, however, was the immediate plight of the woman who had written me. I called her on the telephone. "They tell you to go home and die," she said. "The doctor prayed that I would pass away the third day after the operation. It would be a blessing, he told my mother. He said that I had a malignant blood-vessel tumor and had only two to six months to live anyway. When the lump returned, mother begged him to tell her of any other specialist. She pleaded with him, saying she would sell her house — anything to pay. The doctor replied that there was no one else. That was all they could do; it was up to God now. With this type of tumor, he said, you go quick.

"I wrote to Dr. Gerson, telling him of my difficulty in getting money to continue my treatments and how I had been refused by the Red Cross, the Welfare Department, and all the other charitable organizations. Even the minister of my own church turned me down! The Cancer Society was ready to help me with the payments that I owe the hospital for surgery and treatments until they found out I was going to Dr. Gerson. Then they refused. Now I guess the hospital is going to sue. It's big business!

"I was almost evicted from my home when The Foundation for Cancer Treatment sent me $150, to be repaid at $5 a month, with no interest. The Foundation is a nonprofit organization founded by the ex-patients of Dr. Gerson's out of gratitude.

"I guess society wants me to die of cancer. They would rather I died than to be cured the 'wrong' way!"

Next I called a very famous cancer research organization which has collected untold millions of dollars in gifts from the American people.

"On the thousand to one chance that this woman is right," I suggested, "that she is supposed to be dead and that, contrary to medical science, she remains alive through the treatment of this Dr. Gerson, couldn't you see your way clear to give her $50 a week for a year?"

They denied that Dr. Gerson's treatment was of any value. If the woman wanted to go to a bona fide hospital and receive bona fide treatments, they would help her, they said.

"But she already has," I said, "and they can do no more for her. They sent her home to die!"

They were sorry, they said, but that's the way things were. My informant took me into his confidence, buddy-to-buddy style. He was very jovial, and he spoke patronizingly of Dr. Gerson. "The thing is," he said, "Dr. Gerson doesn't talk about the ones he *doesn't* cure!"

That was a strange statement to make. It presupposes that Dr. Gerson *has* cured people of cancer! But everybody knows you can't cure cancer with a diet.

Or can you?

Armed with the results of my investigation, I decided to confront Dr. Gerson with the evidence.

CHAPTER THREE

A quack, I felt, would do one of two things. He would refuse to see me, or he would do just the opposite — roll out the royal rug of welcome and charm me with stories of the wonderful things he had been doing with cancer, hoping that I would return to my office and write a glowing account of his accomplishments.

Dr. Gerson did neither. His secretary told me he was busy with his patients and could not talk to me. A few days later I tried again with the same response. I was impatient. Mentally, I had Dr. Gerson pictured as a small, dark, ferret-faced man — the kind of cancer quack you see on television — who had a "good thing" going for him and was terrified that the press wanted a word with him about one of his patients. Naturally he wouldn't want me prying into his affairs.

But I was wrong. A week later his office called and informed me that Dr. Gerson would see me.

I was wrong again about his appearance. He was an old man! But he was tall and spare, with blue eyes and white hair, and spoke with a German accent. He was neither eager nor reluctant to answer my questions. As a matter of fact, I asked very few questions. It was he who did most of the talking. Very early in our discussion I got the impression that Dr. Gerson had been all through this before. Not once, but many times. But kindly and patiently he endured my comments, many of which, I'm afraid, were not well-founded. I am not a medical writer and have never claimed to be, and Dr. Gerson was willing to go along with me — up to a point. Then he exploded. "Can't you understand that this type of cancer has never been cured?" he yelled. "That never in the history of medicine has such a patient been cured!

That she is well now and working. Here, here are the X-rays. I will explain them to you!"

Later the 77-year-old doctor smiled. "They do not like for me to cure cancer," he said. "They say it is not possible. I say it *is* possible, and I do it!"

But why had he been reluctant to reveal the details of his treatment, as charged by the American Medical Association?

For a reply, Dr. Gerson showed me letters of rejection from various medical magazines:

Samples: *New York State Journal of Medicine*, Feb. 9, 1943: "I regret to inform you that the New York State Journal of Medicine is unable to avail itself of your article entitled 'Cancer: A Deficiency Disease' for publication."

Medical Record, Dec. 7, 1944: "We are returning, herewith, your paper on 'Dietetic Treatment of Malignant Tumors' as we cannot see our way clear to publish it. I would suggest that you send it to one of the journals devoted to the subject of cancer, as it is more in their field than in ours."

The cancer research organization that I had called had told me that "there are accepted channels for a doctor to go through to publish a new theory." But here, these "accepted" channels had apparently been closed to Dr. Gerson. Why? Was the diet-cancer theory too unorthodox?

Nevertheless, he had published fifty medical papers and three books. It didn't sound as though he were reluctant to reveal anything.

"If they want to know any more about my diet," said Dr. Gerson, "tell them to look in their library. They have a copy of my book, *A Cancer Therapy,* in which the diet is plainly outlined!"

At this point I had on my hands a "quack" who had no mysterious drug to sell and no secret treatments — only a completely unorthodox cancer therapy.

Where did the "ill-gotten gains" come in? Doctors who treated cancer the ordinary way certainly weren't starving to death, by any means. Why the need for a new method unless — unless he believed in it! And Dr. Max Gerson looked to me like a man who believed what he was saying. He was shy, a little awkward because the English words did not come easily to him, but a man of obvious dedication and integrity. I doubt if a quack would have shouted at me like that! He would have been too anxious to make a good impression on a reporter.

The story that I had already written in my mind about Dr. Gerson was coming apart. Now I was not so sure. I could not afford to jump to quick conclusions, especially since those conclusions would be read by many hundreds of thousands of people in my newspaper. I needed facts, many more than I had now. But one thing was certain: I was no longer on the smooth, the even, and the direct way to my story. I was chasing down one of the hundred byways.

"Five times," Dr. Gerson was saying. "Five times they sent a committee here to investigate my methods, the Medical Society of the County of New York. I let them see patients, X-rays, records, everything."

This was a break for me! Here were people who knew medicine. Their findings would certainly indicate one way or the other whether Dr. Gerson's treatment was of any value.

"What were the results of those investigations?" I asked eagerly.

"I do not know," he said. "They have not revealed them."

No newspaperman would like that last statement. Even less would he like it in view of the gravity of the problem. Why had they not revealed the findings? If they found that the doctor's therapy was useless, shouldn't they make this information public? Didn't they have a moral obligation to do so? And weren't they as morally obliged to publish the news if Dr. Gerson was actually curing cancer? I did not like the unwarranted secrecy surrounding a matter that concerned every man, woman, and child living, a matter of desperate importance to cancer sufferers and their families.

I learned something else before I left Dr. Gerson's office. I learned that he had been suspended from the Society because of his appearance on the Long John radio program in New York, an appearance arranged for him by an overanxious member of the Foundation for Cancer Treatment. The program is an all-night discussion program which uses no scripts. Therefore, it is easily possible to make a slip, to say something you will later regret. Though this makes for interesting listening, it can backfire on the speaker.

Long John, a well-known radio personality, has had many M.D.s on his program, but they have not been suspended, nor have they elicited the hundreds of letters and telephone calls that descended upon the station during and following the show.

"No, I don't regret the program," Long John Nebel informed me, "but that was two years ago, and I've learned a lot since then. Today, I would insist on another M.D. with the opposite viewpoint being present."

I spent a Saturday afternoon in Kew Gardens, New York, talking with a very gracious and charming woman, Mrs. Johnna Oberlander, eldest daughter of Dr. Gerson and secretary of the Foundation for Cancer Treatment. I was inspired by her devotion to her father's ideals and by her cheerful courage in the face of opposition to the doctor's crusade. She explained that the Oakland Manor Cancer Clinic at Nanuet, N.Y., had been discontinued in March, 1958.

"My mother felt it was getting too much for the

doctor," she said. "He's 77 now. Some of the best cases were started there, where the diet could be administered under professional supervision."

I asked Mrs. Oberlander about the special chopping and juicing machines which the American Cancer Society said were offered to the Doctor's patients for sale at around $150.

"Dr. Gerson has nothing to do with the juicer. I do. He knows I can explain it to the patients and felt it would be helpful to demonstrate it to them. It's immaterial to him where they get it. Many get it from dealers in their own cities. We also have it for convenience, so that I, knowing his work, can explain it to them."

She invited me to come into the kitchen and observe the machine in operation. I watched while vegetables were converted into a fine pulp, and then into juice.

"It seems quite a reasonable price for the machine," I said.

"It is when you consider that X-ray treatments run $25 and up. Many hospitals could not exist but for these treatments and the income they bring in. It takes the average person about $6,000 to die of cancer. This machine is useful and can't do any harm, while the X-ray is questionable at best."

I asked her if she expected a medical breakthrough from organized medicine in its war against cancer.

"There's always a 'breakthrough' announced around cancer contribution time. It is almost as if it were more profitable to look for a cancer cure than to find one!"

She told me that Dr. Albert Schweitzer was one of the directors of the Foundation, which is today mainly educational, and that Dr. Gerson had cured Schweitzer's wife of tuberculosis of the lungs with his diet.

"She was just over 50 when she came to Dr. Gerson," she said. "The climate of Africa had given her the lung condition. Dr. Schweitzer was extremely grateful for what my father did. He said, 'My wife wouldn't be here today if it hadn't been for Dr. Gerson.' Mrs. Schweitzer died this January at the age of 79."

Being especially fond of salt, I asked Mrs. Oberlander if a saltless diet wasn't most unappetizing.

"I have grown up without salt," she smiled. "When food is prepared the correct way, it retains the natural mineral salts. Taste is retained. You only taste food for a few seconds, but it stays in your body for days. Which is better?"

When I left Mrs. Oberlander's house I had a clearer picture of Dr. Gerson's work. Was cancer really not a disease, as she had told me, but a symptom of a disease? Was it possible to cure cancer, not by cutting and burning the cancer itself, but by treating the whole body, by rebuilding it with fresh, natural foods? Did the diet work?

To prove or disprove it, I knew I had to have the results of the five investigations made by the Medical Society of the County of New York. If the findings were negative, I could continue my investigation of a "cancer quack." But if they offered promise that Dr. Gerson's cancer therapy did indeed have value — that was something else again. And if that was true, a legitimate question would present itself.

Why weren't the findings revealed?

CHAPTER FOUR

An article about Dr. Gerson in *Herald of Health Magazine* suggested to me that it would be no easy job getting hold of the results of those investigations. Read one paragraph: "At no time have reports of the committee been available. They were not published by the New York Academy of Medicine, nor have inquiries to the Academy been acknowledged or answered."

Would they be as high-handed with the press, I wondered?

My letter to the Society went as follows:

"We have not yet published a story concerning Dr. Max Gerson because every organization we have contacted says that it does not pass upon the efficacy of a doctor's treatment. They further explain that there are channels through which a doctor can go to present any new treatment, and that Dr. Gerson has not done this.

"From the Foundation for Cancer Treatment I learn that Dr. Gerson has repeatedly tried to go through these proper channels, and each time has been rebuffed. His articles have been rejected, and apparently he has no other way to turn. I understand that a committee of doctors from your society has investigated Dr. Gerson on a number of occasions — seen X-rays, examined patients, etc. — and that none of these findings has ever been made public.

"We have no feelings one way or the other concerning Dr. Gerson's treatment except that of public responsibility. Is there any way we can be advised of the nature of your findings?"

This was their reply: "As you can readily understand, all proceedings before the Medical Society of the County of New York are of necessity, and by their very nature, privileged on behalf of the doctor concerned.

"However, if you will write to Doctor Max Gerson and ask him if, in the event he would like us to release the information you are seeking, he will communicate with us in writing, requesting that we submit these findings to you, we will be glad to do so. Any request for release of material of this kind must come directly from the doctor."

This seemed a sensible enough letter. I understood their viewpoint completely. All I had to do now was to get Dr. Gerson's permission. Who said it was going to be difficult?

Dr. Gerson found it hard to believe. I couldn't resist feeling a bit smug that I had pulled it off so easily. The doctor then wrote out a letter authorizing the Medical Society to turn over to me the results of the investigations. Already I had consumed several months on the story and was eager to wrap it up. It wouldn't be long now.

How wrong I was! Back came a letter from the Medical Society: "This office has received a letter from Max Gerson, M.D., authorizing us to release to you the results of our investigations.

"The results are that Doctor Max Gerson was suspended from the rights and privileges of membership in this Society for a two-year period."

I was stunned! The door had been slammed shut in my face! *The results are that Doctor Max Gerson was suspended from the rights and privileges of membership in this Society for a two-year period.* I delved into my files and brought out their first letter to me. The last paragraph read: "Doctor Gerson is a member of this Society but is presently under suspension from the rights and privileges of membership, *as a result of personal publicity.*"

This was confusing. Was there some connection

between "personal publicity" and the investigations? Was the Society irked because of the educational literature put out by the Foundation for Cancer Treatment? I knew that sort of thing was frowned upon, and I could understand that the Society, anxious to preserve its good name, might be peeved about it.

I wrote them another letter: "I assume that you have changed your mind and do not intend to release the information to me as you promised. I did not need an authorization from Dr. Gerson to learn from you that he has been suspended; you told me that the first time I wrote to you about him. Then, however, you told me he had been suspended because of unfavorable publicity. Now you tell me it was a result of your findings. If you will not send me the results of your investigation, can you not send them to Dr. Gerson himself?"

Their answer went like this: "We received from Doctor Gerson a letter giving you the authorization to receive from us the results of the several investigations referred to in your letter. You will note that we are authorized through this letter by Doctor Gerson to give you the results of the several investigations. This we have done."

Yet, their first investigation had been made a dozen years ago, the last in 1954. Why had they waited so long before suspending him? Did they want to make sure they were being perfectly fair to him? But since his suspension in March, 1958, more nearly coincided with his appearance on the Long John radio program a year earlier than it did the protracted and intermittent investigations ending in 1954, it was easier to understand the Medical Society's first letter to me — that Dr. Gerson had been suspended because of personal publicity.

I was stymied and perplexed for the moment. Let's assume, I thought, that all the investigations were unfavorable to Doctor Gerson, and that the Medical Society, after thinking it over, had decided not to damage him by releasing the results to the press. That made sense enough, but I had suggested that they send the results directly to him, not to me. Who would be damaged? It would then be up to Dr. Gerson's discretion whether he wished to turn over the findings to me. It would seem that a doctor who had been investigated on a number of occasions certainly had the right to know the result of the findings!

Suppose again, I thought, that the investigations proved a very definite value in Dr. Gerson's treatment. What is the logical question to ask? Why weren't the findings released not only to Dr. Gerson, but to the whole world?

But suppose again that the investigations proved, to the Society's satisfaction, that Dr. Gerson's therapy did neither harm nor good. Most of his patients were terminal cases, for whom nothing more could be done anyway — and Dr. Gerson did give them hope, which was something.

In an attempt to reinforce this last assumption, I wrote again to the AMA: "Thank you for your reply to my letter concerning Dr. Gerson. You mention that you commented on Dr. Gerson, and his reluctance to reveal the details of his treatment, in an editorial in *The Journal.* 'Therein it was pointed out that although Dr. Gerson has been requested to do so, he has failed or refused to acquaint the medical profession with the details of his treatment.'

"I understand that Dr. Gerson has published fifty medical papers and three books, including *A Cancer Therapy,* Dura Books, Inc., New York. I have a copy of that book, and to a layman's eyes at least, Dr. Gerson's complete regimen is explained. Further, I understand from the Foundation for Cancer Treatment that Dr. Gerson has been trying for years to 'go through proper channels' and acquaint the medical profession with his findings. Apparently, all his articles come back from the *Journal* rejected. I learn also that on five separate occasions a committee of doctors from the New York Medical Society has investigated Dr. Gerson, his patients, X-rays, etc., and not a word of this investigation has been made public. It seems at this time — without my having got to the bottom of the matter, I'm sure — that Dr. Gerson has virtually begged to have responsible persons evaluate his treatment.

"We are motivated only by a sense of public responsibility, and if it can be shown that Dr. Gerson's treatment is worthless, we stand ready to scrap the story. Further, we do not intend to run the story unless we can prove Dr. Gerson's treatment definitely does have value."

The American Medical Association was apparently tired of the whole argument:

"We note your reference to running a story on Dr. Gerson, but that you do not intend to run it unless you can prove that his treatment definitely does have value.

"If you will take Dr. Gerson's word for it, you will have no trouble in 'proving it.' If, however, you desire information on Dr. Gerson, you may wish to check with the American Cancer Society, which might be able to fill you in.

"If Dr. Gerson had anything of value to offer to the medical profession, it would have been utilized long since."

There it was at last, the frank expression of organized medicine's true feelings about Dr. Gerson. Maybe they were just doing their job, protecting the public. Maybe Dr. Gerson, relatively new to this country, was sincere but just didn't know the rules. And maybe there was some connection between his radio appearance and the investigations. Both may have been reasons for his suspension, since the investigations may have been inspired by his publicity.

I had no doubt that these were good men, acting in good faith, but so — I was beginning to believe — was Dr. Gerson.

CHAPTER FIVE

Next I moved into Dr. Gerson's background. I needed more clues, I needed a sense of direction. And amid the welter of contradiction and controversy, I needed all the help I could get.

In the 79th Street Public Library in New York City I found a book called *Master Surgeon*, written by Ferdinand Sauerbruch. Sauerbruch, who pioneered thoracic surgery and was the first to operate successfully on the human heart, revealed an early phase of Dr. Gerson's life.[1]

"I was sitting in a train traveling from Munich to Davos, where I had once again been invited. It had been an exhausting day and I tried to sleep, but in vain. I had probably drunk too much coffee. Grimly I leaned back and tried to read the medical journals I had with me. After we had crossed into Switzerland, another traveler got into my compartment. The man seemed bored, and it was plain that he was looking for a chance to open conversation. He irritated me by shuffling his feet, twitching his legs, fidgeting with his clothes, and by his general restlessness. Before long, he made his opening move.

" 'Are you going to Davos, too?'

" 'Yes,' I growled.

"After a very short silence, he tried again. 'Are you a patient?'

" 'No.'

"He peered across to try and read the titles of the periodicals which I had thrown down beside me on the seat.

" 'So you are a doctor going to Davos?'

" 'No, I am not.'

" 'Thank God for that. Doctors are fools. All but one.'

---

1. Reprinted through the courtesy of Thomas Y. Crowell Company, New York.

"We rattled on through the night. I was desperately tired. I could not read, my eyes were aching, yet in spite of myself I was curious concerning this exception. It was not difficult to set him off again. As I stared at him, he asked, 'What can you see on my face?'

" 'Burns,' I suggested.

" 'Burns!' he cried. 'These aren't burns. They are the scars of skin tuberculosis, and I was cured of it by this doctor.'

" 'What!' I exclaimed, though with some restraint. Skin tuberculosis, lupus, an unsightly disease for which there was no known cure. I decided that my fellow traveler was just bragging. 'There's no cure for lupus.'

" 'There used to be no cure,' he replied. 'But one has been found. I have been cured.'

"Before he realized what was happening, I was unfastening his jacket and shirt, for we were alone in the compartment and some distance from the next station. And on his chest I saw large areas of perfectly healed lupus. I asked him to tell me his story. From his accent, I judged him to be Russian.

"The disease, he said, had developed in his home country; he had gone from doctor to doctor. Being well-to-do, he had been able to afford treatment abroad and had visited various German hospitals — in vain. Feeling more and more like a medieval leper, he had been on the brink of suicide, when he was told that there was a doctor named Gerson in Bielefeld who claimed to be able to cure lupus. He decided to go to him. Why not? The effects of the disease on his face were such that he would soon be forced to retire from the world. People shrank from him, and few hotels would admit him.

"As soon as Dr. Gerson saw him, he exclaimed, 'Ha! Lupus, lupus vulgaris.'

" 'Can you help me?'

" 'Of course I can help you.' And he did.

"I asked him how he had done so.

" 'By diet.'

"In the whole range of medical literature, there was no reference to the treatment of lupus by diet.

" 'When I was cured,' he continued, 'I went to all the famous doctors who had told me there was no cure, and they all laughed at me. Doctors!'

" 'Did you ever go to Sauerbruch?' I asked.

" 'It wouldn't have been any use. He's in Munich, and anyway, he always quarrels with everybody, shouts and bellows at them. He wouldn't listen.'

"I told him that I knew Sauerbruch and that I could guarantee that Sauerbruch would see him. And then he told me why he was going to Switzerland. He was hoping to acquire a building for the treatment of lupus patients free-of-charge. It was to be a gesture of gratitude for his release from this dreaded scourge. But he knew that he would need the support of some prominent man, for Dr. Gerson's name was practically unknown.

" 'Do not forget to call on Sauerbruch,' were my parting words to him. 'I shall see that you are received by him.'

"About a fortnight later, the Russian was shown into my office, accompanied by a modest man with a highly intelligent face. Dr. Gerson himself, I guessed.

" 'So you were Sauerbruch yourself!'

"Gerson declared that he had cured a number of patients by excluding salt from their diet entirely. My Russian visitor was one of them. And of his cure there could be no doubt, however amazing his claim might seem. I could see no apparent connection between treatment and cure, but that did not prevent me from beginning a series of experiments immediately.

"I put my assistant, Dr. Hermannsdorfer, in charge of a wing of the clinic which was fitted up as a lupus station. The patients were to be fed in accordance with Dr. Gerson's diet. Lupus patients were found. We securely barred doors and windows to prevent escape. A person who, over a long period, is given food with no salt at all suffers from his situation.

"Dr. Gerson returned to his practice and I promised to keep him informed of our progress. Results were catastrophic. We kept the patients locked up for weeks. Not a grain of salt went into their food, but there was no trace of improvement. On the contrary, in each case, the disease advanced according to rule. Dr. Hermannsdorfer and I were at a loss, thinking of the Russian who had been cured, and of humble Dr. Gerson in whom we had put complete faith.

"We felt we must drop the experiment. Sadly I wrote to Dr. Gerson, telling him of the failure of the experiment and our decision to close the lupus ward. I dictated that letter in the morning. That afternoon, a sister called me to an emergency case: a patient had a severe post-operative hemorrhage. I hastened along corridors and down stairs and did what was necessary. Pensively I was strolling back along the corridor near the lupus ward, when I saw a nurse, the fattest nurse in the building, carrying an enormous tray loaded with sausages, bowls of cream, and jugs of beer. It was four o'clock in the afternoon, hardly the time for such a feast in a hospital. In amazement, I stopped and asked her where on earth she was going with all that food. And then the whole story came out.

"'I couldn't bear it any longer, Herr Geheimrat,' she explained. 'Those poor patients with skin T.B. The stuff they are given — no one could eat it.'

"She was astonished when I dashed her tray to the ground. It was one of the occasions when I completely lost my temper. Every day, at four o'clock when no one was around, she had been taking the patients a nice, appetizing, well-seasoned meal.

"I sent off a telegram to Dr. Gerson, asking him not

to open the letter I had written him. We were back at the beginning again, and from that moment we took extra precautions in guarding the lupus wing. In comparison, a prison would have been a holiday camp. Soon, Dr. Gerson was proved right. Nearly all our patients recovered; their sores almost disappered under our very eyes. In this experiment involving 450 patients, only four could not be cured by Dr. Gerson's saltless diet."

Before Dr. Gerson developed his treatment for lupus, the disease was incurable.

Today, 30 years later, lupus is still considered incurable! At least in the United States, if I am to believe an article written by a doctor in my daily newspaper. The doctor observes that lupus appears to be increasing and names a number of drugs which seem to have some effect on it. But, he laments, there is no cure for lupus.

If there is any possible explanation for this, part of it might lie in Dr. Gerson's own experience. As a young specialist in internal and nerve diseases, Dr. Gerson suffered from an inherited migraine condition. Plagued by pain, dizziness, and nausea, he sought help from the top men in German medicine. Their answers were identical: "Nothing can be done."

To a scientist, those were fighting words. The young doctor plunged into research. He found himself being led down the avenue of nutrition, and there, by trial and error, he evolved a diet that brought him complete relief. The flat tired slogan, "Nothing can be done," really meant, "Nothing *had* been done."

Dr. Gerson began to use his new therapy on his migraine patients and was jubilant to see the same results. But even more specatcular was his discovery shortly afterwards when a migraine patient, whose job was in jeopardy due to his repeated absences, begged the young doctor for help. Dr. Gerson noticed the disease which was eating away the man's eyelids, cheek and nose — lupus vulgaris. Nothing could be done for that. Or rather, nothing *had* been done. At any rate, the man's migraine was more important now. Dr. Gerson prescribed his diet and sent the man home.

Not long afterwards the patient returned. "And how is the migraine?" the doctor asked.

"Gone, all gone!" happily exclaimed the man. "I haven't missed a day of work since!" He couldn't control his excitement. "Doctor, do you notice anything else? My face?"

Dr. Gerson leaned closer. Was it possible — the same man?

"Yes, it's true," said the patient. "My lupus — that horrible, ugly lupus — vanished! Like a miracle!"

It was hard to say who was the more elated — doctor or patient. Would the old disfiguring scourge of lupus also respond to the migraine diet?

Before long, lupus patients were flocking to Dr. Gerson's door, clamoring for the miracle they'd heard talked about. And wonder of wonders, the blessing repeated itself!

Other doctors, who had been echoing the ageless shibboleth of organized medicine, "Nothing can be done," were infuriated with Dr. Gerson's success. They brought charges against him for treating skin diseases, which was not his specialty.

"I'll be very proud to be punished for curing lupus," Dr. Gerson told them.

He continued to cure lupus, and by 1928 he had compiled his findings. Newspapers and magazines throughout Europe hailed the discovery, and offers from many countries descended upon the young doctor.

The bitterness of the medical fraternity knew no bounds. "It is not scientific!" they cried.

"My answer is very short," was Dr. Gerson's reply.

"If it is not scientific to cure people, to cure the incurable, then I am not scientific!"

Why the outcry? Because even then it was more profitable to look for a cure than to find one. Nevertheless, the outcry was soon drowned out by the voice of the people, the one mighty voice invariably triumphant. The people can be deceived, can be butchered and poisoned and cheated for ages without seeming to object, until one voice of protest goes up from the multitude, and then another, and another, until a mighty roar sweeps across a continent.

But they saw there is no cure for lupus. You will perhaps not be excessively concerned about that — unless you had it. Or unless a loved one was suffering from it.

CHAPTER SIX

The most important question of all was whether Dr. Gerson's cancer therapy worked. It was therefore imperative in my investigation that I find patients who had benefited from the treatment. This would not be easy, for professional ethics forbade Dr. Gerson to reveal the names of his patients.

At this time I came across an illuminating article published in the *Our Town* newspaper of Maywood, New Jersey. Titled "Benny and Joe — 'Miracle on Pleasant Ave,' "[1] it was the beautifully written and inspiring story of a man apparently condemned to die of cancer until, in desperation, he turned his back on organized medicine which had offered him nothing but more suffering and death.

MIRACLE ON PLEASANT AVENUE

The story of Benny and Joe could well be titled the "Miracle on Pleasant Avenue." This wonderfully human story with two local merchants playing the lead roles is years old — suddenly brought into focus this month by the publication of a book called *A Cancer Therapy* which is soon going onto the shelves of the Maywood Library.

The book, written by Dr. Max Gerson, describes a strikingly effective treatment of cancer and outlines in detail the case histories of 50 patients. Case No. 42, which starts on page 368, is the clinical story of Joe Panebianco, who owns and conducts the Maywood Bicycle Shop (63 West Pleasant).[2] Amply illustrated by a sequence of X-rays, which shows marked improvement even to the untrained reader, the text tells of a remarkable story in cancer treatment and recovery.

1. Reprinted through the courtesy of Len S. Rubin, Editor, *Our Town*.

2. Only initials of patients are used in the book.

The story is a long and rich one, filled with innumerable details, each of which means much. But the human element swirls around the names of Benny and Joe, two barbers. It is a story which touched the despair of having a specialist give up hope, of watching cancer work its horrible daily toll — and a story which reaches the peak of seeing a miracle come true, a tale of recovery which seems so impossible that even today there is the feeling of unreality about the years which have passed.

The crux of what eventually happened revolves about the driving insistence of Benny the Barber that the manager of his barber shop, whom he could see being slowly destroyed by the scourge of cancer, visit a certain doctor about whom Benny had heard much but never met.

A year went by before Benny Comp's faith brought Joe to the office of Dr. Max Gerson. At this stage, Joe Panebianco was apparently dying, given only a brief time to live. Today he still operates the bicycle shop he had established as an additional enterprise just before being afflicted, only a few doors from where Benny still runs his barber shop.

And Joe Panebianco's family, without hesitation, gives full credit to that last desperate gamble, the visit to the doctor they knew so little about and a cancer therapy which wrought wonders in a matter of days — a miracle within a year.

The story of Joe Panebianco dates back to the fall of 1953 when he was working as manager of Benny's barber shop and his family operated the small bicycle shop some doors away. He suffered a loss of voice, continual coughing. There was little concern. The homemade diagnosis was laryngitis. The voice failure persisted and he began the visits to doctors which turned up the information that a tumor had formed on the left lung.

Joe stopped barbering, dropped out of Rotary — and the long bout with the disease started. The tumor was found inoperable and he started a series of deep X-ray treatments which brought great improvements. Under the probing heat, his voice was regained.

The honeymoon was shortlived. By November, 1954, his left leg began to pain, lose feeling. By January, some 16 months after the first warnings, there already seemed no hope for Joe Panebianco.

He found great difficulty in breathing (the tumor had increased upon his lung), he could not sleep nor turn his neck without great pain — he could hardly walk.

His wife, who has been the most wonderful source of inspiration through the years of trial, spoke to the specialist in NYC. She asked if Joe was strong enough to make a trip to Florida, something he very much wanted.

And as Mrs. Panebianco recalls so vividly, the doctor said, "Let him go anywhere he wants in the few days he has left." (That same doctor, when called two years later for back X-rays for Joe Panebianco, asked with astonishment, "Do you mean to say that he is still alive?" He asked to see Joe and made a careful review of the case, the comparison of negatives, the treatment, etc.)

The trip to Florida was brief, as the physician had warned. Joe was in such agony throughout the trip, so progressively worse that the Panebiancos, who were traveling by car with other members of the family, started back immediately after arrival. They drove 17 hours without stopping in a desperate try to reach home in Paterson with Joe still alive. Today, he recalls that he never thought he would survive that gruelling experience.

They arrived home on February 19, 1955. On Sunday,

his former boss, Benny, rang his doorbell. He was back, for another in a ceaseless string of pleas to get Joe to see Dr. Gerson. A year earlier Benny had cancelled all appointments in his shop and called to take Joe to the doctor's office. He failed to impress the Panebiancos with the importance of visiting this specialist in the treatment of cancer. Benny repeated the information gained from one of his customers. He was convinced that Joe had to see this Vienna doctor with offices in NYC and a home for patients in Nanuet, N.Y.

That time, in 1954, Joe held back. This time there was no saying no. All other physicians had given up. On Sunday they drove to Nanuet.

After the kindly, elderly physician had examined Joe and explained the method of treatment, the length of time Joe would have to stay in Nanuet, etc., Joe worried himself to his feet and started towards the door.

"We'll think about it," he managed. Doctor Gerson took his hand. "There's nothing to think about," he said, "You must stay."

And he did. Dr. Gerson explained to the family that there was an incredibly sized tumor on the lung. Larger than a baseball, it was a threat to Joe's living out the rest of the week. The cancer had spread elsewhere. His legs, with muscles destroyed, were extremely weak.

The Gerson therapy is a simple thing, revolving around diet. Emphasis is placed on the deteriorated metabolism as a whole with the liver as its central organ. As John Gunther described it, in his deeply moving book, *Death Be Not Proud,* the story of his own son's death by cancer:

"The Gerson diet is saltless and fatless, and for a long time proteins are excluded or held to an extreme minimum. The theory behind this is simple enough. Give nature an opportunity, and nature herself will heal. It is the silliest thing in the world to attempt to arrest cancer of the tongue, say, by cutting off the tongue. What the physician should strive for, if he gets a case in time, is to change the metabolism of the body so that the cancer dies of itself. The whole theory is erected on the basis that the chemistry of the body can be so altered as to eliminate disease."

Dr. Gerson made no promise to the Panebianco family, no wild claim. He said it would take a week before he could determine how his treatment was taking hold. The first few days of the Gerson treatment are extremely difficult. A long series of enemas, as many as five a day, are given in order to totally wash out and cleanse the system. It is a gruelling experience but it opens the way for the restoration of bodily tissues through the introduction of natural foods.

The first week in Joe's recovery was a nightmare of anguish.[1] After five days, coughing spells and chest pains were reduced although other pains increased, in Dr. Gerson's text, "to terrific intensity, lasting almost 10 days."

It was about then, when the pain subsided, that Dr. Gerson first informed the family, "I believe we will save Joe."

He was right.

This remarkable man, who came to this country many years ago and is known in Europe for his great contribution in effecting cures of tuberculosis of the skin, makes no claim of the cure — all nature. Reserved in his predictions he was honest with the Panebiancos and the final result was one of almost full recovery. Today, Joe is just now giving up the use of a cane but his left leg, weakened in the initial stages, is not strong

---

1. ". . . none of the neighboring patients could sleep as he was crying and moaning day and night." Dr. Max Gerson, *A Cancer Therapy.*

enough for full usage. Instead of barbering, he today tends a bicycle shop which permits time off his feet. He works at his trade, repairs, sells, talks bicycles. The tumor on his lung disappeared — as have his fears.

After the cleansing of the system, the Gerson method depends on diet, a rigid, unrelenting diet which casts aside almost all foods but those grown naturally. The diet is potassium-rich and sodium-free. Banned are all foods canned, frozen, bottled, seasoned, smoked. No meats, eggs, fish. No cream, butter, any fats.

Joe subsisted then and to a major degree subsists today on a diet of vegetables and juices, everything freshly prepared several times a day.

His early diet consisted of a breakfast of oatmeal, prunes and orange juice, a lunch of vegetable salad, baked potato, a cup of soup made of fresh vegetables, and a fresh fruit. Supper was the same.

In addition, however, during the day there were nine juices to be taken. These were juices composed of carrots and apples, crushed to a liquid, a green-leaf juice, which contained the liquid pressed from lettuce, red cabbage, parsley, watercress, green pepper, Swiss chard and apples, and straight carrot juice.

Mrs. Panebianco has been a devoted nurse and through the years has prepared the special meals for her husband, at the store during the day and at home evenings. The diet has changed as Joe has improved. The juices have been reduced from one every hour to four a day; Joe has recently had an occasional steak and chicken.

Gerson's diet, as explained in his book, eliminates salt, tobacco, sharp spices, tea, coffee, cocoa, chocolate, alcohol, refined sugar, refined flour, candies, ice cream, cake, nuts, mushrooms, soy beans and soy products, pickles, cucumbers, pineapples, and all berries.

The writer of this article visited Gerson's home in Nanuet and was intensely impressed by what he observed. A normal number of patients was there, approximately a dozen. Each had a fascinating story to tell of hope, in most cases a remarkable recovery.

There was a gentleman from California, given up to die with cancer of the bone, who was preparing to return home after a month's treatment, a changed person. There was a young West Virginia mother of three, who had rebelled against a 10th operation for tumors, and had come to Gerson. In less than a week she had found new hope, had experienced the disappearance of a large tumor. In speaking to this woman, we were left without a doubt as to the genuineness of what had taken place.

The home was a strange place, tenanted by people on the brink of death (for, unfortunately, most of Dr. Gerson's patients are those of last resort, mostly terminal cases) and yet there was hope in the faces. It was a serious place, but there was a positive glimmer of restrained happiness.

The saddest note of all was the fact that Dr. Gerson, himself, was that elderly a person that one wondered (even as you spoke to the dedicated physician) who would follow in his footsteps. His treatment has not been accepted by the general medical world and yet it has proven itself so many, many times that it must be recognized and perhaps, in the future, it will.

Dr. Gerson's conviction is that the chemistry of our bodies is being changed, at great harm to us. That the foods, the means of preparing foods, the very soil is being contaminated by the stages of civilization. With his selection of diet, he is moving to restore the balance in the system; once that is achieved, he professes, sick cells can be restored, cancers can disappear.

Dr. Gerson does not claim to be a miracle man, far

from it. He is joyous when he achieves full success, concerned when he fails. A physician of many years, he has founded a philosophy, put it into medical practice, and has devoted the remainder of his life to bringing this therapy to the world.

His theory has frequently restored life to broken bodies. In the case of Joe Panebianco, he has given him back an existence. To many, Dr. Gerson stands as a beacon of hope.

And the story, in relation to Pleasant Avenue, is that Benny the Barber wouldn't take "No" from Joe Panebianco, his manager, in relation to seeing a certain doctor in Nanuet.

After reading the article above, I put through a call to the Panebiancos. I wanted to hear for myself first-hand what had happened. And, truthfully, I half-hoped that the story I would hear would differ from the article, that I would learn something which would confirm my normal doubt that Dr. Gerson could cure cancer. It is so easy, so comforting to believe in blacks and whites, to have faith and feel secure in the "system." When one man is wrong and the world is right, there's little to fear. He can be ignored, he can be ridiculed, he can be rendered impotent in a number of ways. And you and I are content and satisfied that we are on the winning side.

But let the one man be right and the world wrong — then how can you deny the uneasiness within you? Can you still feel secure? Can you still feel you're on the winning side? After talking with Mrs. Panebianco, I was not so sure. This is what she told me December 12, 1958:

"Every bit of the article is exactly the way it happened, every bit."

"How is your husband nowaday?"

"Wonderful! The only thing is, it affected his leg and

he can't go out and earn a living, a good day's living, because it had affected his leg and he (Dr. Gerson) told us when we started with him that what muscles were damaged, were damaged. He said, 'I don't know how much power he'll get back in his leg,' although they are a little better. He walks a little better and the muscles are a little stronger. But otherwise, the rest of the health is all right. In fact we saw the doctor Wednesday for a checkup since May, the last time we went. We saw new X-rays, which were marvelous. They just had a lot of scar tissue; there was no tumor."

"What were you told by your original doctor?"

"I was told that he had — January of 1954 was when they told him he had maybe six months to live. 'If he gets deep therapy treatments,' he said. 'Of course I wouldn't even bother wasting all that money because they're not going to do much good,' he said. 'He may live a year — maybe.' So we didn't take it for sure, and went to another specialist in New York — in fact he was at Doctors Hospital in February of 1954, and they gave him another bronchoscope. Also the same thing: inoperable, and treatments may do something for him. So we did get treatments and, well, he got his voice back, but it only lasted two or three months. By fall of the same year it started affecting his leg. He went back to the first doctor who gave him six months to live, and he said, 'Well, nothing to do.' He said, 'It's coming into the holidays. Go home and come back after the holidays.' We took him to the hospital again. They tapped the spine to see if it had gone to the spine because it had affected his leg. They said, 'Well, we can't find a tumor there, but nevertheless you're getting worse.' He said, 'Well, what should I do at this time?' They said, 'Just go home and see what happens and wait.' I said, 'Can't we give him more treatments?' You know, you're so excited you'll do anything. He said 'No.' Right now he couldn't. 'The only thing I'll tell you is that before long he'll be paralyzed completely from the right side and won't be able to walk at all.' Well, it was something 'wonderful' to look forward to. So we went to Florida three or four weeks after he'd come out of the hospital, and we had to come home sooner than we had scheduled because he was getting worse rapidly — he couldn't turn his neck, the pain was terrible, he couldn't take a breath. But when we got home this friend of ours came over again and said, 'Look, please, listen to me and try this doctor. If you don't want to do what he wants you to do, don't do it, but only give yourself a chance.' He wanted to take him the year before. We just thought it was ridiculous. How could he do anything? So we went — and that's the result. It's a wonderful thing. I even told my doctor. I said, 'Look, what would you have done? My husband had nothing to lose. We had gone through so much already. Wasn't it worth trying to save his life?' He said, 'I don't blame you, and if this thing is doing him good, you just stick to it.' He was really big about it."

"That's a real success story, isn't it?"

"Oh, as far as we're concerned, it is. And I know of other cases that were there when my husband was there. We correspond with them, and they're also doing well. One special case, 11 years old, a little girl — she's also in the book, initials K.N., Minnesota. The child is going to school, playing, riding her bicycle, doing everything wonderfully, and is still on the diet. She's really progressing very well."

I wanted you, the reader, to read these words just as I heard them, and get a glimmer of the large question mark that was already forming in my mind.

And maybe to feel some of the disquietude that I was beginning to feel.

CHAPTER SEVEN

Thanks to Mrs. Oberlander, I was soon able to talk to the mother of a little girl who had received the Gerson treatment. Mrs. Oberlander wrote to her and received her permission for me to call her.

The mother had no objection to my using her name in the story. "The only thing is," she told me, "I wouldn't want curiosity seekers to waste my time because the schedule for Gail is rather rigid. I have no objection if it would help Dr. Gerson and people who are truly interested. As soon as Gail is off her rigid treatment, then, of course, I would have more time to talk to other people."

I decided no real purpose would be served by using the woman's name, and it might possibly interfere with her daughter's schedule.

But Mrs. A. was quite willing to talk. This is what she said:

"I feel that the treatment has been of great benefit to her and that she would not be alive today if we had not had Dr. Gerson. I really believe it, and I don't think I'm fanatical; but really and truly if you knew the entire history and you had the power to go to the former physician before Dr. Gerson and see the X-rays and get the case history — which I wish somebody would do — you would understand what I mean. But I'm sure you'd get a brush-off, and I mean it very sincerely.

"You see, when you have a patient telling what Dr. Gerson has done, then you find they say, 'Oh, that's what *he* said, but that's not really true.' Such as people in my own neighborhood will say, 'Was she *really* that sick? Well, it just can't be that she's improved this much.' People aren't willing to accept anything other than the orthodox treatment for cancer.

"A very great possibility of what you will find

among physicians of Dr. Gerson's present patients, patients who have left them and gone to Dr. Gerson — they will deny everything and even destroy the records. Now, when I say this, you will probably think I'm crazy, but I am positive it is right because of my own personal experience."

"One doctor, referring to a patient of his who had gone to Dr. Gerson, told me that if she is cured, it is because of the X-rays he'd given her and not because of Dr. Gerson:"[1]

"Yes, there you are, and that is what you will find constantly happening. That is actually the truth. That is what the orthodox people believe, and they are not willing to believe that Dr. Gerson can do anything. They think he's a fanatic, they think he's crazy, they think he's a paranoid."

"Can you tell me what you were told by the doctor who diagnosed your daughter's condition?"

"Well, in the beginning, he ballyhooed me by saying it was nothing but a benign tumor. It might come back, and it might not come back."

"Where was it located?"

"On her leg, in the lower left fibula. She began to limp and complained about it being very sensitive. Then we had an X-ray as the doctor suggested, and then of course he showed us this thing, which was a teardrop shape with the larger part at the base. He recommended surgery by saying it was just a benign tumor. They did a biopsy, and I'm sure he wrote that eventually in the report to Dr. Gerson, although he killed much of our three-month period of time trying to avoid it before he consented to write to Dr. Gerson.

---

1. "In a pratice of nearly 45 years, I have yet to see a single cancer, save a few semi-malignant epitheliomata, cured by . . . X-ray . . ." — Dr. W. A. Dewey, former professor of Medicine, University of Michigan. *Exclusive*, Nov-Dec. 1955.

"So, anyway, we allowed him to operate in June, 1956. Ten weeks later, in September, the cast was removed and X-rays were taken showing little bone knitting and recurrence of the tumor. And in November the tumor was getting larger, the bone knitting was poor.

"In February the tumor was still larger and getting quite swollen at the base. It was sensitive to touch or even to lie down. He wanted to operate again, but I felt that if the first operation had done her no good, neither would the second. So I took her to Dr. Gerson."

"How old was she then?"

"That was three years ago; she was seven. She's fine now, just fine. When I tell my doctor about her, he doesn't believe me."

Mrs. A. did not talk like a fanatic. Her voice was calm, intelligent, and suffused with a deep gratitude toward the doctor to whom she believed she owed her little girl's life. Here, as with Mrs. Panebianco, I was not dealing with hysteria, nor with the "lunatic fringe." These were ordinary people with good sense who did not believe everything that was told to them, looked around for a better way, and apparently found it.

There were many other such people who refused to go home and die. Five of these were presented in person by Dr. Gerson, December 6, 1955, at an industry luncheon meeting in the Hotel Martinque, New York. The 200 business executives present heard a lecture on cancer by Dr. Gerson and a review of the X-rays and case histories of the five patients:

CASE HISTORY #1 — Mrs. G.G. — Medical History
October 1949: After a routine checkup at Memorial Hospital Cancer Institute, New York, patient was referred to Thoracic Division, Memorial Hospital, for X-rays, followed by bronchoscope and biopsy. Diag-

nosis — plus four malignancy in right lung. Right lung removed, followed by slow convalescence.

March 1950: Showing slow general loss of weight and strength, readmitted to Memorial Hospital for observation.

August 1950: Again readmitted to Memorial Hospital for further observation. Four blood transfusions administered. Examination and test indicated evidence of active spreading cancer. Family told cancer would probably develop in remaining lung and that patient's life numbered months at best. Mrs. G. had high fever for seven weeks following last trip to Memorial Hospital. Lost 15 pounds, now weighed only 97; could not endure further X-ray treatments because of weakness. Shortness of breath increased, confining her to chair, day and night, extreme difficulty in eating.

MEDICAL HISTORY FOLLOWING GERSON TREATMENT

October 4th: Mrs. G. was brought to Dr. Gerson for treatment. Within a few months patient improved and all glands and discomforts disappeared. Weight returned to normal and she was able to take up her housework and all other normal activities. 1957 and 1958.

Follow-up: Continued in good condition.

CASE HISTORY #2 — Mrs. D.S. — Medical History

June 1943: Mount Sinai Hospital, New York, report — Dr. S. "Progressive loss of vision in both eyes observed during 1941-42. Had diplopia which lasted two months. Dimunition in the temporal field of the right eye progressed to complete hemianopsia by March 1943. In April 1943 patient had noted that vision in the remaining half of right visual field was diminshed. Examination in June revealed blindness in temporal field of left eye. There was amenorrhea since November 1942. Patient lost 15 pounds between 1942 and 1943. On admission to hospital, positive findings included moderate pallor of both optic discs, impairment of visual acuity in both eyes, bitemporal hemianopsia with an additional lower nasal quadrant anopsia (incomplete) with the right eye. X-rays showed marked enlargement of the sella turcica, with erosion of the walls of the clinoid processes. Patient was given a series of X-ray treatments with slight improvement of visual acuity, but no change in the visual fields. She was discharged to the referring physician and advised to have the pituitary gland tumor mass removed. She refused. Diagnosis — Exceptionally large tumor mass of the pituitary gland, involving the sella turcica to a great extent. Surrounding bones partially destroyed due to partial destruction of left optic nerve.

MEDICAL HISTORY FOLLOWING GERSON TREATMENT

March 1944: Unconscious, patient was brought to Dr. Gerson in an ambulance and treatment was started immediately; regained consciousness after one week. After two months, patient was feeling better and able to do some housework. At the end of eight months, resumed duties as secretary to husband. Although she has only half of the left retina, she can read and write without disturbance.

Note: Case, with illustrations, was published in: *Medizinische Klinik*, Munich, Germany. No. 5 on January 29, 1954.

1957 and 1958

Follow-up: Patient continues in good health and able to work.

CASE HISTORY #3 — Mrs. V.G. — Medical History Diagnosis — Melanosarcoma, recurrent in left leg and thigh. Biopsy — Melanosarcoma, left ankle.

September 1945: Tumor removed, in Beekman Hospital, New York. Later tumor at original site and left inguinal lymph nodes removed at St. Luke's Hospital, New York. Hopeless prognosis was given patients husband.

MEDICAL HISTORY FOLLOWING
GERSON THERAPY

September 6, 1946: First seen by Dr. Gerson and treatment started. Large black tumor mass observed in left groin about the size of a tomato.

June 1947: No tumor could be found.

October 1948: Had normal pregnancy and delivered healthy female baby. Before treatment, patient unable to become pregnant, but since treatment has remained in normal healthy condition.

Note: This case was published in *Experimental Medicine and Surgery*. Volume VII, No. 4, 1949.

1957 and 1958

Follow-up: Condition remains satisfactory.

CASE HISTORY #4—Mrs. M.N.K.—Medical History

February 1941: Removal of tumor in nose; recurrent tumor mass removed in 1943 and regrowth again removed in 1945.

June 1949: Two tumors removed, one from forehead and one from top of head.

February 1950: Large tumor, size of potato, removed together with middle lobe of right lung. Mother was given hopeless prognosis, as the surrounding area was covered with new nodes. Diagnosis — neurofibroma with rapid growth and development sarcoma.

MEDICAL HISTORY FOLLOWING
GERSON TREATMENT

June 20, 1950: Seen by Dr. Gerson; condition —
12 small tumors all over the body, one at the middle
part of the left upper jaw bone, one at right upper
lateral eye bone (orbita) pressing on the eye lid,
one at right temporal part of the head, one at left
upper arm, two on lower right arm and two on left hip
bone and the abdominal wall. Hearing of the right
ear reduced and right eye partly closed.

June 30, 1950: Most of the tumors were no longer
palpable.

July 30, 1950: All tumors had disappeared and in
the following months most of the operation scars were
absorbed.

1957 Follow-up: Patient married and discontinued
diet against Dr. Gerson's advice as liver function was
only partially restored. She got a recidive — a tumor
in her brain — which was treated at home for four
months. After further deterioration, patient recovered
at the cancer clinic in Nanuet, N.Y. Now in good
condition.

CASE HISTORY #5 — Mrs. D.H.J. — Medical History

1923: Growth on left femur removed and later
removal of recidives from the same spot. Diagnosis —
Myosarcoma.

1924: Again removal of recidives from same spot
and X-ray treatment begun. 1925 — Removal of scar
masses at the same spot. Thereafter, wound had remained open.

1928: Skin grafted on open wound. 1929 — Removal of piece of bone at same place. Wound healed
and remained closed until 1940.

1940: The scar mass ulcerated again; bone inflammation and destruction set in. 1941 — All scar

masses removed and skin grafted. Treatment with penicillin and antibiotics until 1944.

1944: Small bone splinter removed. 1945 — More small bone splinters eliminated. 1946 — Another skin graft attempted; wound remained in status quo until May 25, 1951, when patient fractured leg.

1951: Long metal plate extending over two-thirds of the femur was inserted and fastened to the bone with silver screws at the Medical College of Virginia. The muscle and skin would not heal. 1952 — Removal of necrotic masses.

MEDICAL HISTORY FOLLOWING
GERSON THERAPY

September 1952: First seen by Dr. Gerson, patient was bedridden. There was a large extended ulcer opening nearly the entire length of the thigh. In the depth of the large defect, the greater part of the metal plate could be seen. Secretion of pus was abundant; severe pain. Bursitis in left hip joint; patient could hardly walk with crutches.

March 1953: Entire ulcerous wound closed and healed. Growth of new bone broke two of the metal screws, causing slight pain while walking. Bone and surrounding muscles and tissues have been completely restored, so that plate can now be removed.
1957 and 1958

Follow-up: Metal plate removed in May 1956, re-examined in May 1957, patient in good condition, continues to carry on her normal activities.

Note: This case is particularly interesting as it shows a dozen operations during a period of almost thirty years prior to the Gerson treatment, which was then able to restore a limb apparently destined to be destroyed.

These five cases are included in Dr. Gerson's book,

A Cancer Therapy — Results of Fifty Cases, together with X-rays.

Described in clinical terms, these case histories are impressive, even astounding. But these are real people, like you and me, and one cannot help thinking of the fear, the desperation, the misery, the hope, and the joy — the whole living fabric of human emotion — that lie beneath the measured words of the scientist.

If Dr. Gerson had brought only one back from the brink of certain death, no honor should be spared him. But there seemed to be others — many others, as I was discovering — and still men of medicine turned from him in scorn.

Why?

CHAPTER EIGHT

The editorial in the *AMA Journal* of Nov. 16, 1946, had mentioned Dr. Gerson's appearance before a Senate subcommittee that year. Hearings were being held on "A bill to authorize and request the President to undertake to mobilize at some convenient place in the United States an adequate number of the world's outstanding experts, and coordinate and utilize their services in a supreme endeavor to discover means of curing and preventing cancer."[1]

It was the first time in history that the Senate had honored a physician in this way.

But, as Don C. Matchan wrote in *Herald of Health Magazine,* "The committee report of 227 pages, Document No. 89471, gathers dust in the archives of the Government Printing Office."

I wanted that report and told Dr. Gerson that I was sending to Washington for it.

"They will not send it to you," was his firm reply, and once again the challenge provoked a feeling of exasperation.

"Of course they will," I protested. "I'm a newspaper."

But, newspaper or not, I was informed by a senator's office and by the Superintendent of Documents that there were no more copies left.

Mrs. Gerson finally located a copy for me, and I would like you to read some of it. It is important to keep in mind that the hearings were held in 1946 and bitterly discouraging to realize that nothing has been done. Cancer, the unwelcome visitor, the bearer of sorrows, continues his rounds and widens his territory. First it was only the house on the corner, then the house across the street, and then the house next

---

1. Number S. 1875

door. He is not a stranger anymore in your neighborhood.

Senator Pepper. Now, Dr. Max Gerson, of New York. We will hear Mr. Markel first. Gentlemen, you have heard twice the bell ring for the calling of a quorum for the Senate, so I would like us to make our statements just as brief as possible, and if you could make them orally and file your written statements for the record, it might save time.

Mr. Markel. In the interests of saving time, I have a statement here that I will file for the record.

PREPARED STATEMENT BY MR. MARKEL (DECEASED)

I am in favor of the bill in principle. There are very few undertakings more important than this to which the United States Government could address itself. If my information is correct, between 450 and 500 people die each day of this dreaded disease, in other words, about 165,000 to 175,000 each year.[1] This, of course, does not take into account the tremendous suffering by cancer patients.

Millions of dollars have been and are being spent in cancer "research," and while it is unknown how much of the actual dollar finds its way into research, as compared with other expenses, the amazing fact is that the medical profession is apparently still "researching" on the subject matter of cancer, while there resides in New York City an unassuming physician who has long since passed the period of research on animals and is actually treating and, in my humble opinion as a layman, curing cancer in human beings.

I have seen patients who appeared to me to be so far gone as the result of the ravages of cancer as to

1. More than 250,000 died of cancer in 1958, 260,000 in 1959, and an estimated 265,000 in 1960 and 270,000 in 1961.

be beyond the pale of anything but miracles. These miracles are in fact being performed by Max Gerson, M.D., 815 Park Avenue, New York.

I have seen some of these results.

The wife of one of my friends underwent an operation for cancer at the Walter Reed Hospital in Washington where her breast was removed, and which appeared to aggravate her situation, and it appears that cancer had thereafter spread over her lungs. After a visit in New York for several months under the treatment of this scientist, Dr. Gerson, she has returned to her home in Richmond, Va.; she has gained weight, and, so far as I know is cancer free. She says she has never felt better in her life. Her name is Mrs. W. G. Wharton. Her address is 2806 East Franklin Street, Richmond, Va., and her husband is presently the building inspector for the city of Richmond.

I myself was relieved of a very serious case of osteoarthritis by Dr. Gerson after my own doctor had pronounced my condition incurable.

My only interest in this matter is a humanitarian one, having lost my wife with this dreaded disease, and I feel that the least I can do is to add my voice and such funds as I am able to the eradication of cancer, and I have therefore given freely to various campaigns for research. It appears, however, that some doctors are fighting Dr. Gerson. I can readily understand that when results so fantastic are obtained that such claims can hardly be believable. My quarrel with these gentlemen is the fact that they will immediately say such things are impossible, or the doctor is a fake, without even stopping to inquire what is being done. I have had the same experience with my own doctors, who merely throw up their hands and say that anyone claiming to cure cancer is a fake. While I understand that the medical profession considers it unethical for any doctor to say that he cures any ailment unless that cure has been in effect for five years or more, I understand further that the oldest patient in point of treatment for cancer which Dr. Gerson has, in the United States, is about 4 or 4½ years, and I hope that the good doctors of the medical profession will excuse me, if I as a layman say that I would not deny the results that I have seen on account of six months or so, and I feel that it is worthy of investigation and certainly of further research.

The very fact that the patients treated by Dr. Gerson are living today when they were destined to die three or four years ago, according to the statements of these good doctors who treated them, I say is a sensational result and the least that can be said for it is that Dr. Gerson has accomplished something that no one else in the medical profession has accomplished with respect to the treatment of cancer, so far as I am able to ascertain.

I would hate to think that the antipathy to Dr. Gerson would be in any manner associated with the fact that his treatments are dietary and are not surgical. He does not use surgery or recommend surgery, as I understand it, unless there may be some remote cases.[1] Therefore, if this treatment is effective, as I believe it to be, the public would be relieved of millions of dollars of surgical fees, and I repeat, I would hate to think that such possibilities should incense any of our surgeons, who after all are presumed to be humanitarians as well. Dr. Gerson has no doubt made enemies as the result of his dietary therapy, wherein he does not permit patients to smoke or to drink intoxicating liquors or to consume canned goods

1. "In some cases of external cancers — skin and breast — the local treatment may be sufficient. . ." Dr. Max Gerson, A Cancer Therapy.

and other items which could materially affect trade in that respect if it became universal, and of course it was not designed for Dr. Gerson to "make friends" but rather to treat cancer as the result of the many years of his experience.

I think this new approach is very important since apparently cancer research and the cancer research dollar has been traveling for many years down the same avenue of conventional orthodox research, and apparently those good scientists are unwilling to look at or give credence to anything new. In any event, the discoveries of Dr. Gerson should be carried further, as, in my humble opinion, he has unlocked the door to an avenue of approach to this problem from which a solution will be found.

To my mind it is of outstanding importance that facilities be provided in some manner, so that Dr. Gerson may train other doctors in his technique and that hundreds of thousands may be treated rather than the limited number that he is able to personally attend. It would be a calamity if anything happened to Dr. Gerson with no one left to carry on in this particular field, and I hope that the committee will see to it that in the development of cancer research, dietary therapy will have an important part.

MR. MARKEL. I want to say at the outset that I am here in favor of S. 1875. At first I was constrained to oppose that bill like a lot of other people. There was a general apathy. I think Mr. Perlmutter's committee has stirred up some public interest, but there was a feeling that after 50 or more years, millions and millions of dollars spent, with the helpless feeling upon the part of these victims, that out of it grew nothing that they could lean on, not even a hope, and that it would just be another hundred million dollars down the same rat hole, at the cost of thousands of dollars per "rat." I feel, however, that we ought to do something.

The only assurance that I would like to see is that the commission, as constituted, would be absolutely independent, that it would be willing to do a job of research as the name implies — every avenue of research that lends promise of a solution to this problem. There should not be a closed corporation or a gentleman's club where nothing would be heard from it.

We have present here cancer patients, victims, citizens of the United States, and I do not know who would have a greater right, Mr. Chairman, to express their opinion about the expenditures of public money for this purpose than those people. As far as I know, they are in favor of this bill, but I feel truly that research ought to be what it implies.

Since we have been here 50 people have died of cancer, while we are in this hearing. Money, as stated here, means nothing. We spent billions to destroy people, and probably we can spend a few hundred million dollars for the recapture of life. That is what this bill is designed to do, if it will do it; but I am not in favor, Mr. Chairman, of making the commission the tail to any existing kite. Let them decide what they want to do. Let them adopt their own rules. All they need to be is honest scientists and honest Americans.

Now, what bothered me was, as I said before, millions are being spent for research. We are still researching with animals, while here, an unassuming scientist in New York — and I hope the medical profession will pardon me for using the word "cure" — is curing cancer today.

Now I understand that a patient must have been free of a recurrence of disease for five years before an ethical doctor would be permitted to say the patient was "cured." Well, fortunately, nobody can take my license away, because I am an ordinary layman. I am not a scientist, I am not a doctor — and I will not cloud the results on account of six months: I say when the patient has lived 4½ years longer than the time allotted by reputable doctors, I am willing to say he was cured. At least, he has not been buried when he was designed to be by the hospitals that sent him home to die, Mr. Chairman. They were told that they could not live but a few months. That is four years ago. Something has been done for them. It has not been surgery. It has not been radium. It has not been X-ray — and those are the only three things, if my information is correct, that the millions of dollars had been spent upon. I say, if there is another avenue, a nutritional avenue — which this is — or anything else which gives promise of the cure for cancer, these research artists at least should be willing to condescend to look at it, Mr. Chairman. In this case there have been outstanding scientists, I am told, who have been told of this, and they do not even want to look at it. I do not ask them to admit that it is true. At least take a look.

SENATOR PEPPER. Well, suppose we hear Dr. Gerson. I have been informed by a Mr. Markel and by a gentleman from Florida who is a friend of mine, they have been very much impressed by the work that has been done by Dr. Gerson, and they have requested that he be heard here, at this hearing. I assented to the request. Mr. Markel, I believe we could do better, in view of the short time — and I know you would like to do this — to hear Dr. Gerson as soon as we can.

MR. MARKEL. Yes, and we have Dr. M. here.

SENATOR PEPPER. All right. I have those two. We will hear them just as soon as we can.

STATEMENT BY MAX GERSON, M.D.
NEW YORK, N.Y.

Dr. Gerson. My office and residence is at 815 Park Avenue, New York City.

I am a member of the AMA, Medical Society of New York State, and Medical Society of New York County.

The dietetic treatment, which has for many years been known as the "Gerson diet," was developed first to relieve my own severe migraine condition. Then it was successfully applied to patients with allergic conditions such as asthma, as well as diseases of the intestinal tract and the liver-pancreas apparatus. By chance a patient with lupus vulgaris (skin tuberculosis) was cured following the use of the diet. After this success the dietic treatment was used in all other kinds of tuberculosis — bones, kidneys, eyes, lungs, and so forth. It, too, was highly favorable in many other chronic diseases, such as arthritis, heart disease, chronic sinusitis, chronic ulcers, including colitis, high blood pressure, psoriasis, sclerosis multiplex, and so forth. The most striking results were seen in the restoration of various kinds of liver and gall bladder diseases which could not be influenced by other methods up to the present.

The great number of chronic diseases which responded to the dietetic treatment showed clearly that the human body lost part of its resistance and healing power, as it left the way of natural nutrition for generations.

The fundamental damage starts with the use of artificial fertilizer for vegetables and fruits as well as for fodder. Thus, the chemically transformed vegetarian and meat nourishment, increasing through generations, transforms the organs and functions of the human body in the wrong direction.

Another basic defect lies in the waste of excrements

of the cities. Instead of returning the natural manure to the fruit-bearing soil, it is led into the rivers, killing underwater life. The natural cycle is interrupted and mankind has to suffer dearly for the violation. Life in forest and wilderness should teach us the lesson.

But we can regain the lost defense and healing power if we return as close as possible to the laws of nature as they are created. Highly concentrated for speedy reaction, they are laid down in the dietetic treatment.

(Dr. Gerson placed on file with the committee a pamphlet entitled, "Dietary Considerations in Malignant Neoplastic Disease.")

DR. GERSON. The tuberculosis treatment was tested with favorable results in Munich, Kassel, and Berlin. A demonstration was scheduled in the Berlin Medical Association for May 5, 1933, but I left Germany for Vienna after the political upheaval, March, 1933.

The fist cancer patient (bile ducts) was treated in 1928 with success. Seven favorable cases followed out of 12 and remained free of symptoms up to 7½ years.

In Vienna I tried a modification of this treatment in six cases of cancer without any result.

After two years I moved to Paris where a patient, Mr. Horace Finaly, president of the Banque de Paris, bought a clinic for continuation of this treatment. There I had three favorable results and one undecided case out of seven cases of cancer, following the use of the Gerson diet.

In New York I started the Gerson diet in cancer patients, 4½ years ago in 1941.

The evolution of the dietetic treatment is given in detail in one article published December, 1945, and another one will be published soon.

The treatment is inaffective in cases with less than 10 lymphocytes in the differential blood count when the phosphorus cannot be brought back into the red blood cells and other tissues; it is also ineffective in patients with advanced liver damage, and, of course, in those who are in extremis.

Since the end of January, 1946, I treat my patients in a hospital in New York, a number of them without charge, and never refuse any patients, irrespective of their condition, in order to see what this treatment can do for them. Up to the present all practical and research work was financed by myself in cancer, as well as other chronic diseases, including tuberculosis and I will not ask for money, here. This limits the progress of the method.

My experience leads me to believe that the liver is the center of the restoration process in those patients who improve strikingly. If the liver is too far destroyed, then the treatment cannot be effective.

Aware of the imperfection of this as well as any other theory, I shall try, nevertheless, to explain the end results of the Gerson diet. It is condensed in three surpassing components:

(1) The elimination of toxins and poisons and returning of the displaced "extracellular" Na-group, connected with toxins, poisons, edema, destructive inflammation from the tissues, tumors, and organs where it does not belong, into the serum and tissues where it belongs — gall bladder with the bile ducts, connective tissue, thyroid stomach mucosa, kidney medulla, tumors, and so forth.

(2) Bringing back the lost "intracellular" K-group combined with vitamins, enzymes, ferments, sugar, and so forth, into the tissues and organs where it belongs: liver, muscles, heart, brain, kidney cortex, and so forth; on this basis, iodine, ineffective before, is made effective, continuously added in new amounts.

(3) Restoring the differentiation, tonus, tension, oxidation, and so forth, by activated iodine, where

there were before growing tumors and metatases with dedifferentiation, loss of tension, oxidation, loss of resistance, and healing power.

(Dr. Gerson placed on file with the Committee a document entitled "Case History of Ten Cancer Patients, Clinical Observations, Theoretical Considerations, and Summary.")

SENATOR PEPPER. Proceed.

DR. GERSON. I would like to show you a few of the patients.

SENATOR PEPPER. All right, we would be glad to have them.

FIRST CASE

DR. GERSON. This is Miss Alice Hirsch.

(Dr. Gerson presented for the record the following operative record:)

NEWARK BETH ISRAEL HOSPITAL
OPERATIVE RECORD

Name: Alice Hirsch. Age: 14. Date: October 15, 1945. Preoperative diagnosis: Spinal cord tumor.

Surgeon: Dr. William Ehrlich. Service of: Dr. William Ehrlich. First assistant: Dr. Wolfson. Anesthetist: Dr. Dear. Anesthesia: Endorrachial Ether. Suture nurse: Miss Goldberg. Procedure: A midline incision was made extending from the spine of C-7 to D-3. The spines and laminae of D-1 to D-3, were removed with rongeurs. The dura did not pulsate. On opening the dura the cord was found to be swollen and had a yellow appearance. There were several tortuous varicosities on the surface of the cord. On compressing the jugulars no fluid could be obtained and consequently, the laminectomy was extended upward in two stages until the spines and laminae of what are estimated to be C-4, C-5, C-6, and C-7 were also removed. Here, too, the dura was tense, and on opening it the cord in this region had a glistening reddish-gray appearance as if it was completely infiltrated with gliomatous tissue.

The cord bulged through the opening in the dura. Exploration laterally and anteriorly was carried out to be sure we were not dealing with an anteriorly placed extramedullary tumor. A fine needle was inserted into the midline of the cord but no cystic fluid could be obtained. Inasmuch as the patient had fairly good motor power in the lower extremities, it was not deemed advisable to incise the cord for biopsy.

The dura matter was left open for decompressive purposes and closure was completed using interrupted No. 1 chromic catgut in layers for muscle and fascia and interrupted black silk for subcutaneous tissue and skin. The patient stood the procedure well and returned to her room in good condition. Post operative diagnosis: Cervical and upper thoracic intramedullary glioma.

Style of operation. Laminectomy, C-5 to D-3.

DR. GERSON. This original statement shows that this was a cervical and upper thoracic intramedullary glioma. This is the only case now at least arrested in 2,000 years of medical science. The patient was operated, she being a girl of 15 years old.

(Dr. Gerson presented as a witness before the subcommittee at this point Miss Alice Hirsch, of Hillside, N.J.)

SENATOR PEPPER. What is your name?

MISS HIRSCH. Alice Hirsch.

SENATOR PEPPER. And what is your address?

MISS HIRSCH. 558 Sweetland Avenue, Hillside, N.J.

SENATOR PEPPER. All right. Now, what did the little lady have?

DR. GERSON. She had intramedullary glioma. Glioma is a tumor of the whole cerebral nervous system; it could be in the brain or in the spinal cord, and this was in the spinal cord. You can see they operated here, by the scar. They took the bones out for inspection. They made a so-called laminectomy.

SENATOR PEPPER. You made the operation?

DR. GERSON. No. It was made in the Newark Beth Israel Hospital; date, October 15, 1945.

SENATOR PEPPER. That is where the operation occurred?

DR. GERSON. Yes. Here is the original operative record.

SENATOR PEPPER. What did you do?

DR. GERSON. The physician told the father: *We cannot do anything; it is a tumor, and nobody can remove such a tumor from the spinal cord. She would die.*

SENATOR PEPPER. Was that before the operation?

DR. GERSON. No. During the operation they saw that the tumor was in the spinal cord, inside — not outside. An extramedullary tumor can be removed; so they operated to look into it and to see whether it was extra or intra. When they found it as an intramedullary tumor they could not do anything — closed, and sent her home, and told the father, 'Please make her as comfortable as possible; that is all; we can do nothing else.' Then she came to me, and we applied the treatment. She had a paresis in the lower right arm; the process involved especially the nervous ulnaris of the right hand. She could not walk much, both legs became more and more paralyzed, little by little, increasing while the tumor grew. It destroys the spinal cord and stimuli from the brain cannot be carried to the muscles which atrophy.

SENATOR PEPPER. And by your dietary treatment you cured the tumor?

DR. GERSON. We killed the tumor, yes; otherwise, you can understand, the muscles could not have been restored; she can now move the hands and arms. Maybe there is a little bit of weakness left here. Professor Howe was much interested in this extraordinary case.

SENATOR PEPPER. You gave no treatment except your dietary treatment?

DR. GERSON. She had some liver injections, too.

SENATOR PEPPER. How long was she under your care?

DR. GERSON. She is still under my care.

SENATOR PEPPER. How long ago was it she came to you?

DR. GERSON. The end of October.

SENATOR PEPPER. Of last year?

DR. GERSON. Of 1945.

SENATOR PEPPER. Is the statement that Dr. Gerson has made, substantially correct?

MR. HIRSCH. Absolutely. She was to have been paralyzed by around December 1; she was supposed to be, according to the other doctors.

SENATOR PEPPER. What was her condition when she went to Dr. Gerson?

MR. HIRSCH. Very, very weak.

DR. GERSON. She could not walk.

MR. HIRSCH. We had to feed her by hand. We had to take her up out of bed when she wanted to go anywhere, and she could not walk to any extent.

SENATOR PEPPER. Could you see the tumor?

MR. HIRSCH. No.

DR. GERSON. No.

SENATOR PEPPER. It was inside; was it?

DR. GERSON. Only by the operation is it visible.

SENATOR PEPPER. Did the doctors who operated at this Newark Beth Israel Hospital tell you they could do nothing about the tumor?

MR. HIRSCH. That is right.

SENATOR PEPPER. And that there was a tumor in the spine?

MR. HIRSCH. We knew before the operation that

there was a tumor in the spine, and before the operation it was almost impossible to do anything for her.

SENATOR PEPPER. Is this a true copy of the report of the Newark Beth Israel Hospital about the operation and all?

MR. HIRSCH. That is right. That is from the Beth Israel.

SENATOR PEPPER. Would you like to leave a copy of this for the record?

DR. GERSON. I have presented that for the record.

SENATOR PEPPER. Dr. M, do you know also about these cases?

DR. M. Yes. I have seen all these cases many times. I have been watching it for the last six to eight months, depending on how long they have been Dr. Gerson's patients.

MR. MARKEL. Dr. M. will file a statement for the record.

SENATOR PEPPER. Did you know about the case of Miss Hirsch, who was here, before?

DR. M. Yes. We had a neurological consultation on Miss Hirsch, since I saw her, because I felt I was not a capable enough neurologist to make any decision whatever on Miss Hirsch's condition, and we had Dr. Hubert Howe, of the Neurological Institute, Columbia University, see her, and we had her, the last few months, and I have a statement here by Dr. Howe in relation to several patients that he has seen at Dr. Gerson's.

SENATOR PEPPER. Are you a medical doctor?

DR. M. Yes.

SENATOR PEPPER. From what school did you graduate?

DR. M. Northwestern University Medical School.

SENATOR PEPPER. Are you a member of the American Medical Association?

DR. M. Yes.

SENATOR PEPPER. And is it your opinion as a doctor that the cure, or the apparent cure, or improvement in the condition of Miss Hirsch which you witnessed, is due to the treatment that Dr. Gerson gave her?

DR. M. Well, I cannot see anything else to account for it. It is the only change in routine which she has had at all. If it were an isolated case you would say, "Well, maybe she was going to get better, anyway!" But if she had died, as apparently everybody who saw her thought she was going to die, everyone would have said, "Well, you see what happened!" But taking it along with quite a few other cases, it is no longer a coincidence.

SECOND CASE

SENATOR PEPPER. Let us take the next case, here. What is your name?

MR. GIMSON. George Gimson.

SENATOR PEPPER. Where do you live?

MR. GIMSON. 729 Thirty-second Street, Union City, N.J.

SENATOR PEPPER. Dr. Gerson, tell us about Mr. Gimson.

(Dr. Gerson presented for the record the following letter:)

VETERANS ADMINISTRATION
Lyons, N.J., November 26, 1945

DR. MAX GERSON
New York, N.Y.

DEAR DOCTOR: In compliance with a request from the above-named veteran we are submitting the following information.

First symptoms of present illness were present about May, 1944. First symptoms in the Army since induction. First Army hospitalization was Regional Hospital, Fort Riley, Kansas, August 28, 1944, treatment above.

Examination is not remarkable except for a freshly

healed scar. However, review of the entire block of tissue removed, shows that histologically the malignant areas have been removed completely. Orthopedic examination reveals patient evidences extreme pain on all body motions even remotely related to the back. All back motion is limited by pain. Straight leg raising produces lumbar pain. Obers sign is positive, prone thrust produces pain referred to the lumbrosacral region. All reflexes are normal. X-ray taken October 10, 1944, shows cervical spine in normal alignment and shows no bony abnormality, except a spina bifida occulta of the seventh cervical segment.

Treatment here consisted of extensive physiotherapy to back, dressings to the neck, and heat treatment to right ear.

Condition on completion of case: 1. Unimproved. 2. Cured. Disposition recommended: Since this patient's hospitalization he has complained of low back pain. He has been given an extensive course of physiotherapy with no signs of improvement. In view of these findings, a CDD discharge is recommended.

Maximum hospital benefits have been attained. No. 1 diagnosis is considered to be permanent. No. 2 Not permanent.

Diagnosis: 1. Strain, ligamentous, lumbrosacral, moderately severe, secondary to injury incurred in fall, April, 1943, Federal Shipbuilding & Drydock Co. Kearny, N.J.
2. Carcinoma, basal cell, skin back of right neck, of hair follicle origin and precursor of rodent ulcer.

Very truly yours,
R.C.F.

DR. GERSON. Mr. Gimson came with a big tumor that was arrested. He was operated first when he was a soldier and was in camp.

MR. GIMSON. Fort Riley, Kan.

DR. GERSON. And then they operated, but they

could not remove the basal cell carcinoma, because it was grown up into the skull, so they sent him for deep X-ray therapy to another hospital.

MR. GIMSON. Fitzsimmons, Denver, Colo.

DR. GERSON. He was sent to Fitzsimmons Hospital, at Denver, Colo., for deep X-ray therapy, but there they decided that deep X-ray therapy is very dangerous to the brain, and the specialists there refused.

MR. GIMSON. They did not give me any treatment at all, so they discharged me.

DR. GERSON. They discharged him and sent him out and told him, "Sorry, we can't do anything!" Then it grew further, and the whole face was swollen. His left eye was entirely closed, he could see very little with the right one.

MR. GIMSON. This one is still swollen. You can see the crack.

DR. GERSON. And I sent the case also to Professor Howe, the neurologist, and he saw it was growing into the brain, and caused all these disturbances; and I have some X-rays and all other things, there, but I do not know whether to put them on the table.

SENATOR PEPPER. He came to you, and you treated him?

DR. GERSON. Yes.

SENATOR PEPPER. And you applied your diet?

DR. GERSON. Yes.

SENATOR PEPPER. And did you give him any liver injections?

DR. GERSON. Yes, daily, at home. I think his wife gave them to him.

MR. GIMSON. Yes; that is right.

SENATOR PEPPER. And what is this, that you have here?

DR. GERSON. That is from the Veterans Administration, the original.

SENATOR PEPPER. This is a letter that purports to be

from the Veterans Administration, at Lyons, N. J., dated November 26, 1945, addressed to Dr. Gerson, and signed by R.C. Fagley, Major, MC, Chief Medical Officer. It purports to relate to George J. Gimson, C-4491792. That is the serial number, and the letter purports to be a report to Dr. Gerson about Mr. Gimson's illness.

Now, Mr. Gimson, you tell us about the case. What was your condition, and what treatment did you get from the Army? When did you go to Dr. Gerson, and what did he do? And what relief have you had?

MR. GIMSON. I went to Fort Riley, Kan., and I had something like an ingrown hair, you might say, on my neck. I went down to the hospital, and the doctor, the major, looked at me, and he told me, "Have it off; it wouldn't take long," and I could be back with the troop, and I wouldn't lose any time, I would be back in a day or two.

SENATOR PEPPER. How long were you off?

MR. GIMSON. I was off 4½ or 5 months. Two days I had marching, to keep us busy, out of trouble. Then I went to the hospital. Down there they told me I would be back with the troop in two or three days. I went down and had the operation; the next morning, and I wound up in bed, and I could not move my head or anything — pulled away over on the side. They came in for inspection. This captain came in one morning and told me it was about time I had my head straightened out. I told him I could not move my head, because from the operation it pulled me all over on the side, so he just straightened it up, and he opened it all up again; and when he ripped it open like that, I told him, "I can't feel anything; I can't hear anything," so he looked at me, and he checked me, and he gave me an examination; then he told me, "We are going to send you," he says, "to Fitzsimmons, Denver, Hospital." I asked him, "Why should I go there? Why couldn't I go east?" He said, "Well, we haven't got the right equipment here for what your trouble is, so we are going to send you out there."

SENATOR PEPPER. Where were you?

MR. GIMSON. I was in the regional hospital in Kansas; and from Kansas they shipped me out to Denver, Colo., to Fitzsimmons, and when I went to Fitzsimmons they gave me an examination and took a hypodermic needle and stuck me in the head with it to see if my feeling was there, so I did not have any feeling whatsoever, and they were going to give me this deep X-ray therapy, and they did not give me any. I put in for a Christmas furlough, and that was refused to me, so then they gave me a discharge the following week, and when I came home the tumor was coming up. Half my white shirt is all worn on one side from where this tumor swelled up behind my ear, where the scar was. It had started to come up again, so I went to the Red Cross about it, and I told them I could not sleep at nights, and I had pains; I could not even do a day's work. I would have to quit as soon as I put any pressure on myself; so she sent me down to Lyons, N.J.; so I went down there, and they told me they had lost all my papers and records. I guess they did not want to tell me what was wrong; so they told me the only thing they could do for me was to send me to the Bronx, N.Y., and get a specimen; so I asked them, "You mean a specimen by operation?" He says, "Yes." I says, "There is no more operating on me," and I refused all operation, so I came home, and my wife told me I was going over to see Dr. Gerson.

DR. GERSON. Why did you refuse an operation?

MR. GIMSON. Well, they did not do me any good the first time, and my condition was worse; so I went over to Dr. Gerson, and he gave me this book, and that is what I am to do. There is no more tumor.

SENATOR PEPPER. Now, tell us this. Did you stay in the hospital for any length of time?

MR. GIMSON. No.

DR. GERSON. That was before the hospital was established.

SENATOR PEPPER. He gave you this book, to tell you what to eat and what not to eat?

MR. GIMSON. Yes; what to eat and what to drink, and everything.

SENATOR PEPPER. And you went by this diet?

MR. GIMSON. Whatever is in that book, that is what I took.

SENATOR PEPPER. And you followed strictly, this diet?

MR. GIMSON. 100 percent. I gave away my last pack of cigarettes just before I went up to his office, and from that day to this, I never smoked a cigarette.

SENATOR PEPPER. You quit smoking?

MR. GIMSON. I quit smoking, and drinking, too. Last night I was best man at my brother's wedding, and I couldn't even drink.

SENATOR PEPPER. How long, now, did you take this diet before you began to notice any improvement in your condition?

MR. GIMSON. Well, I would say about, oh, a month, two months, a month and a half to six weeks.

SENATOR PEPPER. You took no medicine, or had no other treatment?

MR. GIMSON. No. Liver injections.

MR. GIMSON. Everything I am supposed to take and eat, everything is right there (referring to the little book).

DR. GERSON. Here is the medication book.

SENATOR PEPPER. So you are satisfied the treatment Dr. Gerson gave you has been responsible for the improvement in your condition?

MR. GIMSON. Every bit of it.

SENATOR PEPPER. All right. Thank you.

MR. MARKEL. May I ask Dr. M. to talk about this case?

SENATOR PEPPER. Dr. M.

DR. M. I saw this patient when he had already recovered to a great extent. I saw him after he had been under the treatment three or four months. I have been watching him, seeing him once a month, since. There is no sign of recurrence, certainly, and this particular patient has had a lapse, establishing it as a basal carcinoma, which is sometimes inimical to other treatments, but usually when it involves the bone as it did in this case it has gone pretty far. He had actual bone involvement, and apparently there are no signs of that at present.

SENATOR PEPPER. Was the tumor that he had what we call a real tumor?

DR. M. Yes, it was a tumor, starting with a hair follicle..

SENATOR PEPPER. Was it malignant?

DR. M. Yes.

SENATOR PEPPER. Was the tumor that the little lady, Miss Hirsch, had, a malignant tumor?

DR. M. It is a diffused glioma, which is somewhat different. It comes out of connective tissue and it produces most of its ill effects by actual scar tissue from the glioma surrounding the nervous tissue in the spinal cord itself.

SENATOR PEPPER. Thank you, Mr. Gimson. We appreciate your coming.

THIRD CASE

DR. MARKEL. Who is your next witness?

DR. GERSON. Mrs. Anna Hanna.

(Dr. Gerson presented as a witness before the subcommittee, at this point, Mrs. Anna V. Hanna.)

SENATOR PEPPER. All right, Doctor. Tell us about Mrs. Hanna's case.

DR. GERSON. In the Jefferson Hospital, Philadelphia, an operation was performed on the patient. We found — I read this original.

An extensive carcinoma just above the rectosigmoid with infiltration of the mesentary of the rectosigmoid and descending colon. The growth was adherent to the vena cava and both iliac vessels, and there were suspicious nodules in the liver.

Because of the metastatic involvement, resection of this growth was impossible. I took a specimen for biopsy which proved to be adenocarcinoma. Operative procedure consisted of a permanent colostomy.

That is an original letter first sent to Dr. Jules Vogel, and then sent to me.

SENATOR PEPPER. The letter to which you have referred is the letter from Dr. Thomas A. Shallow, 1611 Spruce Street, Philadelphia 3, Pa., and the first letter was dated April 23, 1945. That is the letter to Dr. Vogel. The other letter is a letter dated June 24, 1946, from Dr. Shallow to Dr. Gerson, enclosing a copy of the letter to Dr. Vogel of April 23.

Now was that a malignant growth?

DR. GERSON. Yes; Carcinoma. When the lady came she was in a terrible condition. She could not eat, and her stool came here (indicating). Now the treatment closed the permanent colostomy. The physicians thought it would be always there, but nature even closed the permanent colostomy, and now her stool goes through the anus, as the tumor is entirely absorbed. We have wonderful X-rays. I have them here. The patient has gained weight and is in good condition.

SENATOR PEPPER. Mrs. Hanna, will you give us your full name and address, please.

MRS. HANNA. Mrs. Anna V. Hanna, 331 Virginia Avenue, Manoa, Upper Darby, Pa.

SENATOR PEPPER. Is what Dr. Gerson has said substantially a statement of your case?

MRS. HANNA. Yes sir; absolutely.

SENATOR PEPPER. Did you take any treatment except the treatment that Dr. Gerson gave you?

MRS. HANNA. No sir, not any; and they certainly came down and told my daughter there was absolutely nothing they could do, she was free to consult anybody she wanted.

SENATOR PEPPER. What doctors did you consult, by the way, about your condition, before you went to Dr. Gerson?

DR. GERSON. Miss Alice M. Hanna, the daughter, went to Dr. Vogel, first. He is the family physician.

SENATOR PEPPER. Will you just tell us a little bit about your mother's case; what doctors she went to, and what they told her?

MISS HANNA. First she went to Dr. Vogel.

SENATOR PEPPER. Dr. Jules Vogel?

MISS HANNA. That is right. And he was suspicious of a tumor in the colon, and possibly cancerous, he said, from his examination; so he sent her to the Fitzgerald Mercy Hospital, in Darby, Pa., for X-ray pictures. These X-rays confirmed his suspicions, and he sent her to Dr. Thomas A. Shallow, a surgeon, of Philadelphia.

SENATOR PEPPER. Of 1611 Spruce Street, Philadelphia, Pa.?

MISS HANNA. That is right. Dr. Shallow placed her in Jefferson Hospital in Philadelphia for examination and treatment, and after eight days of examination and some treatment to build her up he operated on her with the hope that he could remove the tumor; but during the operation he realized that it had grown so extensively and attacked so many organs that it was impossible to remove it. So he performed a colostomy to afford her temporary relief, and the report that he gave to me was that she might live six months, she might live two years—he could not predict the time, and it was very definite that she would not live very long. That operation took place on April 19, 1945.

So while mother was still in the hospital, a girl in my office who happens to be a friend of Mrs. Fleming, another patient who is here today, told me of Dr. Gerson, and I got in touch with Dr. Gerson, and he said that he thought perhaps he could do something for her, but she had to remain in the hospital for two to five weeks. She developed pleurisy and different difficulties, and it was possibly two months following the operation before I could bring her to New York to see Dr. Gerson, and he gave her the regular Gerson diet.

SENATOR PEPPER. Did she go to the hospital?

MISS HANNA. No, she did not, Senator.

MISS HANNA. And we have been going to see Dr. Gerson every two weeks, and since then we have been going once a month to see him.

SENATOR PEPPER. And he then prescribed his diet and then you took her back home?

MISS HANNA. That is right.

SENATOR PEPPER. Did you notice; did your mother begin to improve in health?

MISS HANNA. Almost immediately; and at the end of five weeks I believe X-ray pictures show that the tumor was almost completely gone.

SENATOR PEPPER. You went back to doctors and got X-rays, and they reported?

MISS HANNA. Dr. Gerson takes X-rays, and during all this time she has been under the constant surveillance of Dr. Vogel, and he is very much impressed and thrilled with her response. He says he has never witnessed anything like it.

SENATOR PEPPER. And she has had no other treatment that you attribute her recovery to except Dr. Gerson's treatment?

Miss Hanna. Absolutely none.

Senator Pepper. All right. Thank you very much.

Dr. Gerson. I sent the patient back to Professor Reimann to see her, and sent her back to Jefferson Hospital, and the physicians were so impressed that they demonstrated her to the other students, and even called the case (I wouldn't do it) "cured" — as a cured case. She was demonstrated by Dr. Engel.

Miss Hanna. That is right. Dr. Bucher, pathologist at the hospital, presented her to the Jefferson Hospital medical student body.

Senator Pepper. Dr. Bucher?

Miss Hanna. Dr. Bucher. He is the pathologist.

Senator Pepper. At the Jefferson Hospital, he exhibited her to the students?

Miss Hanna. Yes, sir.

Dr. M. I have not examined Mrs. Hanna recently, but Dr. Reimann and Dr. Kilingle, of Philadelphia, examined her and could find no evidence of a sigmoid-ostomy of any kind, nor of the original growth.

Senator Pepper. Was your mother able to walk around when she went to Dr. Gerson?

Miss Hanna. Just a little bit, Senator. She was practically laid down in a bed in the back of the car to make the first trip, entirely. She did manage to walk upstairs once or twice a day.

Senator Pepper. Thank you very much, and thank you, Mrs. Hanna for coming and giving us your statement.

FOURTH CASE

All right. Now, who is next?

Dr. Gerson. Mrs. Fleming.

Senator Pepper. Go right ahead.

Dr. Gerson. Mrs. Fleming had a lymphatic sarcoma. She had terribly big tumors in the abdomen, glands all over the body, neck, axilla, both groins, two big tumors from rebro-peritoneal glands, and mesenteric glands; and one tumor was removed, there. Biopsy was made by Dr. Ginsberg.

And slides were sent to two other hospitals, to Dr. Stuart, in New York, and another professor, I think Yale, and all three decided that it is a myeloma, more specifically a plasmacytoma, a kind of very bad malignant tumor.

MRS. FLEMING. Dr. Averett removed it.

DR. GERSON. Yes; he removed a piece for biopsy, and the others examined it.

SENATOR PEPPER. Now, let us get Mrs. Fleming. What is your name?

MRS. FLEMING. Katherine Fleming.

SENATOR PEPPER. Will you just tell us what your condition was before you went to Dr. Gerson — and this is Miss or Mrs.?

DR. GERSON. Mrs. Fleming.

MRS. FLEMING. I started several years before, going around from doctor to doctor, and nobody seemed to know what was wrong.

SENATOR PEPPER. And who told you you had a malignant tumor?

MRS. FLEMING. Dr. Leonard Averett, who operated the specimen.

SENATOR PEPPER. And he told you that you had a malignant tumor?

MRS. FLEMING. He did not tell me. He told my people.

SENATOR PEPPER. He told your people that you had a malignant tumor? All right; go ahead now.

MRS. FLEMING. So after I came out of the hospital he ordered X-ray treatments. I took 15 of those, and quit work; and so then he discharged me and told my people there was nothing more could be done, it was just a matter of time; and I went from 165 pounds to 130 pounds, and then they took me to Dr. Gerson.

SENATOR PEPPER. When did you go to Dr. Gerson?

MRS. FLEMING. May, two years ago.

SENATOR PEPPER. And Dr. Gerson gave you his Gerson diet?

MRS. FLEMING. Yes, sir.

SENATOR PEPPER. And did he give you any liver injections?

MRS. FLEMING. Yes, sir.

SENATOR PEPPER. Did he give you any other treatment?

MRS. FLEMING. Just the vitamins.

SENATOR PEPPER. And vitamins? And so, have you had an examination lately? You consider yourself cured, now?

MRS. FLEMING. I was examined by Dr. Averett, January, a year ago, and he said I had no signs of ever having it.

SENATOR PEPPER. You consider yourself cured?

MRS. FLEMING. I think so.

SENATOR PEPPER. And you attribute your cure to the treatment that Dr. Gerson gave you?

MRS. FLEMING. Nothing else; positively.

DR. GERSON. Her leg was terribly swollen.

MRS. FLEMING. My leg was like that. The right leg.

DR. GERSON. Tumor masses pressed on the vena cava, and the leg was blue and terribly swollen, so she could hardly walk.

Now, something else happened. The case is interesting in several other respects. I will make it very short. When the patient was one year under my treatment, because the ovaries were killed for treatment reasons, she had terrible so-called flare-ups, menopause reactions, perspiration and heart palpitation. So I tried to give her an ovary substance; immediately, the ovarian substance brought the tumors back. That is one of the cases where I have now seen that. Immediately, the tumors start to grow. Now, at that time, I found when I gave a little bit of iodine before, I could destroy the tumor so that they cannot grow more. I gave her then for five months Lugol's solution, and after this I tried again to give her different substances to see whether the tumors will regrow again. Nothing happened. I gave her fats, and with fats also I could bring the tumors to regrow; but now, even, we, as physicians, are able to bring the tumors back; they can regrow, but we are able to suppress the tumors; when we give in addition to the treatment a little bit of iodine, no tumors can regrow again.

The first case in this respect, where I made these experiments, is the next patient, Mrs. Beatrice Sharpe. This is the second, then came a third; and from now on I knew a little bit of iodine has to be added — but the individuals react differently, and that has to be worked out scientifically.

MR. MARKEL. Ask Dr. M. if he is familiar with this case.

SENATOR PEPPER. Do you know about this patient?

DR. M. I sent this case to Dr. Gerson, as a test, because a couple of years ago he had made this statement to myself and to Dr. Charles Bailey, of Philadelphia, an outstanding chest surgeon. Dr. Gerson was in Seaview, New York. I went over to see his tuberculosis cases, and some of his results were very, very remarkable. He had several bronchial chest fistulas which had healed up, which had no right to heal, and he had mentioned at that time the possibility of using this in malignant disease. Both Dr. Bailey and I smiled skeptically, thinking it was rather fantastic; so I picked out the worst case I could find and sent him one, which happened to be Mrs. Fleming; and much to my surprise she improved. She was supposed to live three to five months, approximately, and instead, she is still here. The tumors have at least palpably disappeared; they may reappear, but at least there is no evidence now, so far as she is concerned. She has put on very many pounds.

DR. GERSON. Twenty pounds.

DR. M. Her sister is giving constant reports, and she says she continued to improve and she has remained improved. It is two years now since that occurred. Certainly, something should have happened by now if it were going to. We do not know — we are still watching it. She has a two-year improvement, at least.

SENATOR PEPPER. Thank you very much for coming, Mrs. Fleming.

FIFTH CASE

Now, Doctor, have you another?

DR. GERSON. Mrs. Beatrice Sharpe.

MRS. SHARPE. 13553 Two Hundred and Thirtieth Street, Laurelton, Long Island.

DR. GERSON. The patient was first operated three years ago.

MRS. SHARPE. 1940.

DR. GERSON. 1940 — now six years ago. Where was it?

MRS. SHARPE. In Jersey City.

DR. GERSON. Jersey City? And two years later she had a recurrence on the breast, left breast operation, the breast was removed, but how much later — two years about?

MRS. SHARPE. Well, about 1941 I had a recurrence.

DR. GERSON. You were at Memorial Hospital?

MRS. SHARPE. Memorial Hospital, yes; taking treatments. In 1942 I had to go back and had more radium treatments. In 1943 I had X-ray treatments, and in 1944 they told me I couldn't take any more treatments, and that was all they could do for me.

DR. GERSON. They sent her home.

SENATOR PEPPER. Now, I have here in my hand what purports to be a letter written from Memorial Hospital for the treatment of cancer and allied diseases, dated September 27, 1944, and it reads:

At the request of Max Gerson, M.D., 815 Park Avenue, New York, N.Y.

Name of patient: Beatrice Sharpe. Address: 13553 Two Hundred and Thirtieth Street, Laurelton, Long Island.

Admitted: To O.P.D. September 8, 1941. Discharged: . . .

Diagnosis: Patient first examined in breast clinic on September 8, 1941, at which time it was noted that she had no local recurrence but had bulky left supra-clavicular mass. This was treated with radium element pack in September, 1941, patient having received 60,000 mghrs — 8,000 mghrs having been given every other day, with excellent regression of mass. Node discovered in left cervical region in September, 1942. This was also treated with radium element pack for a total of 64,000 mghrs with complete regression of disease.

Disease remained quiescent until July, 1943, when patient developed multiple skin nodules over left chest wall in region of scar and medial to it. Low voltage X-ray therapy given to these regions, patient having received 1,500 r (500 r X 3) to left chest wall anterior and left chest wall lateral. At completion of this cycle two additional treatments (400 r X 2) were given to left chest wall anterior, remained under control until July, 1944, when it was noted coming active as well as the mass in the cervical area. It was felt that these areas could not be treated because of proximity to previously irradiated skin.

Last known condition: ....

FRANK E. ADAIR
Attending Surgeon, Breast Service

DR. GERSON. In the photos of X-rays you can see the big nodules. It was at the upper half of the upper lobe of the left lung, and in the supraclavicular glands where the big nodules were. They disappeared in a short time. In a few cases these nodules and the tumor pain disappear. But it was not so in this case, because here some of the pain resisted and she had also terrible menopause reactions because the ovaries were killed for treatment reasons. She could not stand the pain; finally I started to give her only one tablet of ovarian substance — 5 grain, one a day, instead of giving three or four, which is usual. Generally, I saw if one tablet is given for three weeks, all cancer masses come back. Here, all cancerous glands reappeared — also on the other side. You can see here, on the other side all glands came back, not only more cancer masses on the left side, they are also on the right. I applied again the first treatment. All glands disappeared in three weeks, nothing more was left. Then I gave her iodine for six weeks, and then we gave her again, all ovarian substances we have; we gave her double amounts — later three times the amount.

We gave her, in addition, stilbestrol; then premarin — nothing came back. Then we gave her cancer activating (carcinogen) substances, and I have many other cases where I could activate cancer with certain substances, but could make all disappear later. Then we gave her a raw egg yolk. We know this egg yolk was carcinogen too. I killed three patients, when I gave them a little of egg yolk, half an egg yolk a day, but the poor patient had to die for this. These experiments revealed that the patients respond to the first repetition of the original treatment. It is uncertain whether they will respond a second or a third time.

Now, I gave one ounce of egg substance, and, second, the butter, and third, egg yolks — nothing came back. That was the first case where these experiments were made.

SENATOR PEPPER. That was not malignant? The meaning of the letter is that this is a malignant growth?

DR. GERSON. Yes, a regrowing. The medical reports state that it was malignant both times.

MRS. SHARPE. Yes.

DR. GERSON. The menopause reactions are gone, and now she can work.

SENATOR PEPPER. Mrs. Sharpe, you just tell us about your case, will you? What happened to you after you went to Dr. Gerson? Tell us about his treatment.

MRS. SHARPE. In 1940 I had a mastectomy, and in 1941 I went back and I had a recurrence in my neck, and I was sent over to Memorial Hospital for treatments. In 1942 I had to go back, and in 1943 and 1944 there was nothing more they could do for me. I heard of Dr. Gerson through a chiropractor. He gave me Dr. Gerson's name and I thought I had nothing to lose. My head was stiff. I could not move my neck. I went to Dr. Gerson, and in three weeks' time on the treatment the mass started to disappear.

SENATOR PEPPER. You had what — a tumor of the neck?

MRS. SHARPE. Oh, yes.

SENATOR PEPPER. And after three weeks of Dr. Gerson's treatment it started to disappear?

MRS. SHARPE. Yes.

SENATOR PEPPER. And it finally subsided entirely?

MRS. SHARPE. Oh, yes.

SENATOR PEPPER. And you have no more of the symptoms?

MRS. SHARPE. I am going to business all the time.

SENATOR PEPPER. You attribute the recovery entirely to the treatment that you received from Dr. Gerson?

MRS. SHARPE. Oh, absolutely.

SENATOR PEPPER. Dr. M., have you anything to say about Mrs. Sharpe?

DR. M. I saw her fairly early when she still had some tumor masses. Dr. Gerson was very enthusiastic in claiming they had gone down, and they had gone down partially from the original, but since then they have really gone down much more, and I felt at the time he was a little overenthusiastic about it, but certainly his results today, six to eight months later, since I first saw her, justify the fact that there is certainly a steady subsidence of any signs of recurrence, and she certainly remained clinically better.

OTHER STATEMENTS AND COMMENTS

SENATOR PEPPER. Dr. Gerson, have you had other cases, now, of what we would normally call "cancer?" That is, what they think of as a growth — the ordinary case of cancer?

DR. GERSON. These, here are recurrences of cancer.

SENATOR PEPPER. Is that what we ordinarily call "cancer?"

DR. GERSON. Yes, that is cancer.

SENATOR PEPPER. Is that what she had?

MR. MARKEL. All these cases had cancer.

DR. GERSON. Only that in the spinal cord. That is one without metatasis. All others have metastases, and in metastatic cases it is known in medicine that they cannot be influenced.

SENATOR PEPPER. How many people have you treated for cancer who have favorably responded to your treatment, would you say?

DR. GERSON. I might say 30 percent; but all the most hopeless cases. When we get skin cancers, or beginning cancers, they are easy to treat! Even skin cancer growing into the bones as basal cell carcinoma, which are known in medical science that they cannot be influenced — as Mr. Gimson's whose X-rays show how far it had grown into the skull. Professor Howe was very much influenced when he saw this. This was growing through the bones, and now what is left is a scar only.

SENATOR PEPPER. You said about 30 percent of the cases that you have treated?

DR. GERSON. Yes. I would like if you will discuss this with Dr. M. When I would say some things, then they would think maybe I would exaggerate it. I prefer to underestimate. That is much better.

SENATOR PEPPER. Have you anything to say by way of summary of Dr. Gerson's treatment, Dr. M?

MR. MARKEL. Dr. M. would like to make a statement, if you please, Senator, for the record, with respect to all these things.

SENATOR PEPPER. Can you give me a sort of summary?

DR. M. I will give it, and make this short, Senator Pepper.

SENATOR PEPPER. Let me ask you, Doctor, do you favor the appropriation of public money?

DR. GERSON. I would be for it — not for myself, personally, but for research.

SENATOR PEPPER. I do not mean for yourself. Do you favor generally the objectives of this bill?

DR. GERSON. No. All physicians must have money for research. The most important thing in medicine is research. I am in favor of the bill, of course.

MR. MARKEL. Yes; that is right.

Senator Pepper. All right; now, you tell us, Dr. M.
Go ahead.

STATEMENT BY DR. M., NEW YORK

Dr. M. I wish to congratulate you, Senator Pepper,
on the bill. It is a wonderful thing, and I endorse it
wholeheartedly. I think all of us are here for the same
purpose, regardless of how we approach the subject
of cancer, and what our ideas are. As I see it we are all
in support of you, Senator Pepper. Our only argument
is perhaps in the way that good can be done for
people, and that is not a serious difference.

I feel that the Gerson dietary regime offers a new
approach to the cancer problem. We do know experimentally that diet definitely does influence cancer.
There is a lot of experimental work done to substan-
tiate that.[1] I will run through this statement rather
briefly.

I do not think Dr. Gerson has mentioned what the
diet consists of particularly. The Gerson dietary regime
is quite harmless and consists of a low salt, low fat, low
animal protein and high carbohydrate diet, plus frequent injections of crude liver extract and the oral administration of adequate amounts of minerals and
vitamins to supplement those vitamins missing in the
diet. The diet consists chiefly of large amounts of fresh
fruit and fresh vegetables and does not allow any meat,
milk, alcohol, canned or bottled foods. Tobacco in
any form is prohibited. The diet burns down to an
alkaline ash and in general is a combination of many
well known and approved dietary nutritional discoveries by many other workers. It is reasonable to
assume that the closer one's diet is to nature and the

1. "As you undoubtedly know, there is no evidence at the
   present time that any food or any combination of foods specifically affects the course of any cancer in man." Statement
   by the American Cancer Society, July 8, 1957.

soil, with fresh fruit from the trees and fresh vegetables directly from the garden, the nearer one is to normal health. Primary biochemical investigations by Dr. Rudolph Keller indicate that the use of the diet is soon followed by certain definite electrochemical changes, notably shifts toward normal or markedly unbalanced sodium, potassium, and phosphorous ratios in the blood serum and the body tissues. Dr. Keller, as a result of his investigation of the diet, believes that this type of electrochemical reaction can very well change the entire metabolism of the body in cancer patients. A preliminary paper by Dr. Gerson describes the diet in detail and cites 10 cases of cancer in which it appeared that the Gerson dietary regime favorably influenced the course and symptoms of the disease.

This new approach to the cancer problem is of fundamental importance because it is the first promising method which treats cancer as a systemic disease, that is, a disease of abnormal chemistry of the *whole* body. Heretofore, all efforts to treat cancer have been based upon the theory that eradication of the cancer growth must be performed by surgery, X-ray, or radium without regard for abnormal body chemistry which permits the growth to occur. The reason that surgery, X-ray, and radium have not been a real success in the treatment of cancer is that cancer is primarily a disease of abnormal body chemistry, chemistry which is controlled by organs far distant from the site of the cancer. The Gerson dietary regime is an encouraging attempt to return such abnormal body chemistry to normal.

There are certain definite problems to be overcome before any type of treatment of cancer can be considered partially or wholly successful, problems which are not solved by surgery, radium, or X-ray. *A survey made of cancer cases in Pennsylvania over a long period of time showed that those who received no treatment lived longer than those who received surgery, radium, or X-ray.* The exceptions were those patients who had received electrosurgery — in other words, the surgery with an electrical knife — and lived approximately as long as those who received no treatment whatsoever. The survey also showed that following the use of radium and X-ray much more harm than good was done to the average cancer patient. This is a conclusion which is not generally accepted and is highly controversial among leading cancer workers. It would appear that none of the routine measures employed today to combat cancer is as effective as their proponents would have us believe.

We have made two new approaches to the solution of the chief problems which have to do with the cancer patient, itself. In other words, we are trying to do the best we can for all types of cancer patients or propose something which can be studied over a long time, of some significance.

(1) The abolition of pain has been possible only by the use of narcotics, which are deleterious to any patients' general health when administered over a long period of time. This problem, in my opinion, has been solved more by the Gerson diet than by any other method today. We have observed marked relief of pain in approximately 90 percent of the patients who started the treatment with severe types of pain due to cancer.

(2) The further spread of cancer processes has been apparently retarded by the use of the Gerson dietary regime.

(3) A reduction in the size of the original malignant growth has been observed to occur in certain instances following the use of the Gerson diet.

(4) The reduction of metastases or secondarily disseminated cancers from the original growth has been

observed in certain patients where there was an apparent disappearance of metastatic nodules.

(5) The control of acute pyrogenic (pus-forming) infections in areas eroded by cancer, which is one of the chief causes of death in a cancer patient. These so-called secondary infections are eliminated by the treatment itself and by mild medication.

(6) The acute toxic symptoms, such as nausea and vomiting, which are commonly observed in a considerable number of cancer patients may be alleviated by mild medication.

(7) Hemorrhage due to erosion by cancer masses is a frequent cause of death. Its control is only possible if there is no spread from an original cancer or there is a reduction in the original tumor or its metastases. To date the Gerson diet is of value in the control of hemorrhage only to the extent to which it limits directly the encroachment of cancer masses upon important blood vessels.

(8) General debility, and especially loss of weight, have been frequently overcome by the Gerson dietary regime. As a result many formerly debilitated patients were able to do normal work again.

SENATOR PEPPER. Does the patient sustain any loss of weight from the Gerson diet?

DR. M. The diet, although very low in animal protein, seems to be followed at first by a temporary loss of weight, which is usually due to loss of fluid due to the restriction of salt.[1] I think this salt-free diet plays a big part in the reduction of jell around cancer masses. This is a rather well-known finding, and it is one of

1. "Another young boy in whom we were interested was brought to Gerson by his parents after an amputation had been advised for a bone tumor. Following a prolonged stay at the Gerson place, the youngster was returned home in a pitiable state of malnutrition." Statement by the American Cancer Society, July 8, 1957.

the many things which Dr. Gerson has used, which is known to influence such swelling.

(9) The maintenance of the morale of the cancer patient is of primary importance at all times. When any one or any combination of the previously mentioned eight problems are solved for the individual cancer patient, his or her morale is enormously improved so that the practical solution of one or more of these problems must be accomplished wherever possible regardless of whether the patient is considered a hopeless case of cancer or not. That is a humane way to look at that.

Next we must consider the problems to be overcome in the prevention of cancer. The pertinent ones are, in my opinion, as follows:

(1) The discovery of the various causes of the various types of cancer.

(2) The elimination of the causes as they become known without the tragic long interval between the making of a fundamental discovery and the better understanding of its importance and the full realization of its benefits to mankind.

(3) Generalized education in regard to the various causes of cancer as they become known.

There have been many approaches to determine the causes of cancer. From clinical observations on cancer patients, the Gerson dietary regime, for example, provides a most promising lead. In order to profit from this knowledge, an enormous amount of collateral biochemistry must be carried out intensively on both cancer patients and cancer animals by competent workers who are equipped with science's most up-to-date tools for such work. There are many great institutions doing this work. Prominent among them are the Lankenau Research Institute of Philadelphia, the National Health Institute of Bethesda, Md., Rockefeller Institute, not to mention many others.

There are no special cancer hospitals, as yet, doing this highly specialized work in biology and biochemistry to any appreciable degree though they should be encouraged to do this fundamental work in close relation to their carrying out the well-known and often not too successful routine treatment of cancer by surgery, radium, and X-ray.

The history of medicine is filled with tragic errors which allow such a long time to elapse between the time of discovery of a basic principle and the actual medical application of the discovery for the good of mankind. To quote from a recent paper by Hammett (Science, vol. 103, No. 2685, p. 714):

"Nowhere today is this delay more unhappily evident than in the field of cancer research. The accumulated data of Rous, Shope, Coley, Bittner, Strong, Andervont, Green, Greene, Williams, Taylor, Furth, Twombly, Cowdry, Diller, Bawden, Pirie, Stanley, Wyckoff, Kunitz, and others indicate beyond peradventure the path for getting at something of practical benefit to the cancer patient of the future other than surgery and radium."

Even the newly announced radioactive phosphorous cure of skin cancer, and skin cancer only, does not approach the deeper body cancer problem from a systemic or fundamental point of view but is a step forward in the local treatment of cancer.

It is obvious that the many potentialities inherent in the Gerson dietary regime for cancer patients should be explored and exploited to the fullest extent for the common good. In order that this new and highly encouraging approach to the problem of cancer cure and prevention be utilized on a statistically significant scale by both laboratory and clinical workers alike, sufficient funds must be made available for this work. These observations have become apparent to several distinguished physicians who have witnessed the effects of the Gerson diet on cancer patients and whose signed statements are also herewith enclosed.

Therefore, it is my carefully considered opinion that in view of the success so far and the excellent future promise of the Gerson dietary regime, it would be unthinkable not to give major consideration to these new avenues of approach to the cancer problem in the research program contemplated by bill S. 1875.

I first met Dr. Gerson in 1942, at which time I was interested in the effects of the Gerson diet on tuberculosis. I visited his office in New York City, with Dr. Charles Bailey, outstanding Philadelphia and New York chest surgeon, and we observed several tuberculosis patients who had made remarkable recoveries following the use of the Gerson diet. During this visit Dr. Gerson mentioned to me, for the first time, the potential use of the Gerson diet in cancer, an idea which then seemed rather fantastic to me, but no longer does. In the last four years I have found Dr. Max Gerson to be an honest and ethical practitioner of medicine, interested in bettering methods of treatment, as the result of many years of clinical study of the effects of diet on various disease processes. Since January, 1946, we have extended facilities to Dr. Gerson, for a controlled study and observation of his work by physicians. The results are, in my opinion, most encouraging.

— — — — — — — —

NEW YORK 21, N.Y., June 29, 1946

DR. M.

New York, N.Y.

DEAR DR. M.: In the last six months I have had occasion to observe several patients with advanced cancer treated by the Gerson dietary regime. While all of them did not respond to the treatment, the favorable results in some were very striking, much more so than otherwise could have been expected. I believe that this type of treatment should be investigated intensively and on a large scale as it presents many potentialities for the benefit of the cancer patient.

Sincerely,

J.V.R., M.D.

————————

NEW YORK, June 27, 1946

DR. M.

New York, N.Y.

MY DEAR DR. M.: I have observed several cases of malignancy which have apparently been arrested by the Gerson diet, and I am convinced that every opportunity should be given to the continuation of this research.

Sincerely yours,

H.S.H., M.D.

————————

NEW YORK, June 28, 1946

DR. M.

New York, N.Y.

DEAR DR. M.: For over three years I have been observing the effects of the Gerson dietary regime on cancer patients, and it is my carefully considered opinion that many of these patients have been greatly benefited by this type of treatment. The method should be given an intensive trial, as it offers a new and promising approach to the hitherto unsolved problem of a successful treatment for cancer.

Sincerely yours,

A.L.W., M.D.

————————

NEW YORK 21, N.Y. June 27, 1946

DR. M.

New York, N.Y.

DEAR DR. M.: As you know, I have closely followed the cases of malignancy under treatment by the

Gerson diet, particularly the pulmonary ones. I have been much impressed by the apparent reduction of the tumor in several cases and the marked clinical improvement in many of the others. There certainly is a definite benefit in many instances, and it is my firm belief that the research must be continued along these lines.

With best regards, I am,
Sincerely,

C.P.B., M.D.

SENATOR PEPPER. All right. I will just put it in the record, then. Dr. Gerson hands me a letter from H.F.W., M.D., New York, dated July 1, 1946, reading as follows:

For the last seven years I have shared the same office with Dr. Max Gerson, and in that time I have had the opportunity, not only to observe nearly all the cases treated by Dr. Gerson with his diet, but I have used the latter on my own patients.

The results in some chronic skin diseases, in some types of heart diseases and in some dangerous cases of high blood pressure, were astonishing. In some of my patients the blood pressure that had been up to 170 and 180, went down to 130 permanently, and the symptoms of headaches and dizziness disappeared entirely.

During the last three or four years, since Dr. Gerson paid particular attention to the effect of his dietary regime on benign and malignant tumors, I observed practically all of the tumor cases which he treated. I observed and supervised their X-rays and saw the patients at nearly every visit.

One of the first cases of malignant tumors was a Mr. Baldry (1942) who, after surgical removal of a mixed tumor of the left side of the neck, developed a metastatic tumor of the right lung which was diagnosed by X-ray and bronchoscope. During this treatment the tumor disappeared and there was no recurrence when we last heard from the patient about one year ago (1945).

In 1942 I saw one of his patients who had been operated on for cancer of the tonsils and subsequently treated by radium and X-ray which resulted in an X-ray ulcer about two inches in diameter. There were several metastases in the glands of the neck. Under the dietary treatment the ulcer healed, the glands became very much smaller. After a year the patient left New York. Later I read in the papers that the patient died, two months ago. (1946).

Since then I have observed many cases of primary and metastatic cancer. I saw two patients, each with a colostomy which had been performed because the cancer had completely obstructed the lumen of the sigmoid and rectum.

I verified this personally by barium enemas carried out through the colostomy opening and the rectum.

In one case (H) the colostomy wound closed, and normal passage of the bowels was established.

The other patient, treated for about nine months, has gained weight. I had no opportunity to re-examine him as far as the local condition was concerned. I saw him last three weeks ago.

One of my own patients whom I referred to Dr. Gerson because she had been suffering from cancer of the stomach for half a year is doing well. I saw her four weeks ago.

One of Dr. Gerson's patients, who, upon a laminectomy, was found to suffer from an inoperable malignant intramedullary glioma tumor, has regained the use of her arm which was paralyzed when I first saw her seven months ago. I saw her last two weeks ago.

Among his patients I saw four cases of malignant

brain tumor, one of them metastatic. Two seem to be now perfectly well, both of the others had their failing eyesight partly restored; the progress was arrested.

I saw three women who had been operated on for breast tumors, malignant and verified by biopsy, and who had had a recurrence. In all three the metastatic tumors in the lymph glands disappeared, in one of them, also, a local recurrence.

There were quite a number of failures also, but they were, in my opinion, due to the fact that Dr. Gerson accepted for treatment patients who were so far gone that they were absolutely hopeless, even for the most optimistic observer.

I wish to mention that the dietary treatment is equally effective in benign tumors.

In one of two cases of goiter, the goiter disappeared. In the other two the tumor shrunk to about one-third its size. In the first-mentioned case the diagnosis of malignancy was made in the Memorial Hospital, but the method used is not accepted as reliable.

In a case of Recklinghausen the neurofibromas in the face have practically disappeared.

In a case of myoma of the uterus of the size of a small watermelon, clearly outlined by X-ray films, the tumor has become much smaller.

This statement is not intended to give exhaustive summary of Dr. Gerson's work. It is not a copy of his records but a simple report of my personal observations for which I can vouch.

I am intentionally refraining from entering into the question of the theoretical foundation of this method but only report my personal observation of the facts.

H.F.W., M.D.

— — — — — — — —

SENATOR PEPPER. The witnesses who care to examine the testimony that they have given, as recorded by the reporter, can get access to the testimony in room

249, Senate Office Building, where it will be available tomorrow.

DR. GERSON. Mr. Swing is present.

SENATOR PEPPER. Mr. Raymond Gram Swing, would you care to say anything on the general subject, here, of this bill, or anything related to it?

SENATOR PEPPER. Of course, everyone knows the recognized ability of Raymond Gram Swing as one of our distinguished radio commentators in this country.

MR. SWING. I think this bill is one of the most encouraging expressions of intelligent democracy. I hope that it gets the full approval of Congress. It has an inspired work to do, and I want to say in particular that before I came here today I have seen some of the cancer patients of Dr. Gerson, and I believe that research along these lines is so necessary and so hopeful that I am delighted that you, Senator, have had the heart and the courage to bring the doctor here, and some of his patients; and I thank you for it.

SENATOR PEPPER. Thank you, Mr. Swing. We appreciate your coming.

(End of Dr. Gerson's appearance before the committee.)

On Wednesday, July 3, 1946, millions of Americans heard Raymond Swing's broadcast on the American Broadcasting Company network. To the cancer sufferer, to his family, to everybody who hated and feared the cruelest killer of all, it was a message of almost unbelievable hope:

"I hope I have my values right if, instead of talking tonight about the agreement reached on Trieste by the Foreign Minister in Paris, or the continuing crisis of the OPA in Washington, or President's Truman's signing the Hobbs antiracketeering bill, I talk about a remarkable hearing before a Senate subcommittee in

Washington yesterday on cancer and the need for cancer research in new fields.

"Let me first say that I well appreciate that one of the basic virtues of the modern medical profession is its conservatism. For without the most scrupulous conservatism in the statement and application of medical knowledge, there can be no confidence in the integrity of medical science. But for the very reason that the practice of medicine must be conservative, medical science must be bold and unceasingly challenging. Otherwise, medical science will not progress as it can and must, and will lose its integrity.

"A bill is before Congress, the Pepper-Neely bill, to appropriate a hundred million dollars for cancer research under Federal control. It proposes that the government go in for cancer research with something like the zeal and bigness with which it went for the release of atomic energy, turning the job over to the scientists with resources generous enough to solve the problem.

"This alone would make a good theme for a broadcast, just as an example of the use a great democracy can make of its intelligence and wealth. But the subject has been made peculiarly gripping by unprecedented happenings yesterday before the subcommittee which is holding hearings on this bill, and of which Senator Pepper is chairman.

"He invited as a witness a refugee scientist, now a resident of New York, Dr. Max Gerson, and Dr. Gerson placed on the stand, in quick succession, five patients. They were chosen to represent the principal prevailing types of cancer, and in each instance they showed that the Gerson treatment had had what is conservatively called 'favorable effect on the course of the disease.' That in itself is remarkable, but it is the more so because Dr. Gerson's treatment consists mainly of a diet which he has evolved after a lifetime of research and experimentation. Today, that Dr. Gerson has been curing cancer by a dietary treatment is medically impermissable, for the reason that there must be five years without recurrence before such a statement is allowed. Dr. Gerson has cured tuberculosis and other illnesses, with his diet, but he has only been working on cancer for four and a half years.

"Let me say right away that I am not discussing this Gerson diet as a cancer cure-all. It has produced remarkable results. It also has the failures in its records, which anything as yet unperfected is bound to show. It is not something that offers release from the most rigorous and conservative medical observance in its acceptance and application. Whenever something new and promising comes up in medicine, the temptation of the outsider and even some physicians is to run to glowing superlatives and expect too much from it. But anything that offers even a possibility of treating successfully at least some of the four hundred thousand existing cancer cases in this country is stirring news, no matter how conservatively it is formulated.[1]

"There would be no Pepper-Neely bill to appropriate a hundred million dollars for cancer research if the existing research were coping with the need.

". . . I have spoken about his carefully and abstractly, which is to lose some of the shock and delight of the experience yesterday at the hearing of the Pepper Committee. It is one thing to talk abstractly about chemistry and diet and vitamins and other factors in medical science. It is another to see, as the

1. More than 700,000 Americans will be under medical care for cancer in 1959, and about 450,000 new cases will be diagnosed for the first time. More than 40 million Americans now living—one in every four—will eventually have cancer." American Cancer Society, "1959 Cancer Facts and Figures," New York, N.Y.

Committee yesterday saw, a seventeen-year-old girl, who had had a tumor at the base of the brain, which was inoperable, and which had paralyzed her. Yesterday, she walked without assistance to the witness chair, and told clearly about her case and her treatment. There was a sturdy man, who had been a sergeant in the army, had had a malignant tumor, also at the base of the brain, which had been operated on but needed deep X-ray treatment, and this he could not receive because of the danger to the brain. Yesterday he was the picture of health as he testified, and quite naturally he was proud of his remarkable recovery. There was a woman who had had cancer of the breast which had spread. Yesterday, she was well and testified with poise and confidence.

"A few cases showing such improvement cannot, of themselves, affect the outlook of the medical profession. But they are attested facts and not flukes, and as such they have to be accounted for. And there are many, many more cases which could have been cited. It would seem to be the business of medical research to leap on such facts and carry every hopeful indication to a final, conservative conclusion.

"So the advocates of the Pepper-Neely bill can argue that unless we learn now how to deal successfully with cancer, many millions of persons now living in this country are condemned to die from cancer. A hundred million dollars is little more than a token payment for America to make to avert such a sweep of death, and they can then point to the Gerson dietary approach as a most promising field for research. Already it has achieved results, which while relatively few, are astounding and challenging.[1]

"Dr. Gerson was an eminent if controversial figure in pre-Hitler Germany. He was bound to be controversial because he was challenging established practice in treating illnesses as tuberculosis by diet. He has been assistant to Foerster, the great neurologist of Breslau, and for years assistant to Sauerbruch, one of the great physicians on the Continent. The Sauerbruch-Gerson diet for skin tuberculosis is well-known to European medicine and the account of it is part of accepted medical literature. Dr. Gerson told the Pepper Committee that he had first come upon his dietary theory in trying to cure himself of migraine headaches. Later he treated others, among them a man with skin tuberculosis as well. Dr. Gerson was an acknowledged dietary authority in Weimar, Germany, and was responsible for the German Army, of his time, being placed on dehydrated, rather than canned foods."

But all the hope and promise and excitement were for naught. Today, the Pepper-Neely bill, which might have opened the door to a new life of worry-free health for the present and future generations of the world, which might have saved uncountable lives, itself lies forgotten behind closed doors: a dusty testament of man's eternal folly and a legacy of bitterness for the children of tomorrow.

---

1. "At the time Doctor Gerson testified, he was on the staff of the Gotham Hospital of New York. Today he is not on the staff of any hospital. Once he instructed his associates in his method of cancer therapy. Today he finds it impossible to secure medical assistants. Approching the age of eighty, he now practices alone. For over thirty years he has demonstrated excellent results in treating cancer, his approach is on a highly scientific level, and his credentials are the finest. Yet he has never received a penny to aid in his researches . . . Despite the fact that the Gerson therapy is based on authentic physiology, discoveries in biochemistry and nutrition, it has met the usual blackout. The originator is isolated; the medical journals will not publish his work."

    Natenberg, Maurice: *The Cancer Blackout*, Chicago; Regent House, 1959.

CHAPTER NINE

I was now convinced that my original story — that of the cancer quack — had been demolished by the facts. Here was a trailblazer and a crusader, here was a pioneer and a scientist, but here was no quack. And with that conviction came the strange, disquieting feeling of futility. Thirteen years had passed since Dr. Gerson had been given the opportunity of demonstrating to the American people the new and exciting weapon he had fashioned in the war on cancer, but the people had shrugged, had rejected, had acceded to the age-old soothing voice which said, "Nothing more can be done." The prophet had come and gone.

Meanwhile the graves were filling up with the stern and awful refuse of operating and X-ray rooms, those burned and butchered victims turned out of hospitals to go limping hopelessly toward their final rest. Nothing more could be done for them. They had had their checkups, they had sent their checks, they had traveled the same worn, one-way road to suffering and death.

Dr. Gerson had held out hope to these and millions of others. He was still holding out hope, and I was haunted by the statement made in the subcommittee by Mr. Markel: "It would be a calamity if anything happened to Dr. Gerson with no one left to carry on in this particular field."

That calamity was nearer now, in 1959, in view of Dr. Gerson's advanced age. Unconsciously, I stepped up the pace of my investigation. I did not think for one minute that my small efforts would result in an immediate and dramatic change of heart by organized medicine, or that they would establish beyond doubt the value of Dr. Gerson's treatment. But I did hope I could drive the opening wedge in the door so that other investigators could enter.

Shortly after returning from Washington, Dr. Gerson became involved in a very famous and controversial case — that of 16-year-old John Gunther, Jr., son of the well-known author.

The courageous youngster was operated on April 29, 1946, and a tumor the size of an orange removed from his head. In the event the tumor should continue to grow a huge area of the skull, covered by a flap of scalp, was left open.

It did grow, and soon there was a bulge nearly the size of a tennis ball protruding from his head. X-ray therapy — even shots of mustard gas — had little effect on the brain tumor. There was no hope for this brilliant, good-humored lad who had won the hearts of everyone.

Gunther, in desperation, did everything possible to save his son; but 32 doctors, and among them the most famous specialists in the world, stood powerless while the evil thing which they did not understand continued to grow.

In a tragic and magnificent book, John Gunther tells of his son's heroic fight for life and of the almost super-human patience with which he endured his suffering.[1]

"Meantime we were working on another tack. Not for a moment had we stopped searching. Early in the summer Raymond Swing told me astonishing stories about a doctor named Max Gerson who had achieved remarkable arrestations of cancer and other illnesses by a therapy based on diet. Gerson was, and is, a perfectly authentic M.D., but unorthodox. He has been attacked by the *Journal of the American Medical Association* and others of the massive vested interests in medicine; Swing himself had been under

1. John Gunther, *Death Be Not Proud*, Harper & Brothers, N.Y., reprinted by permission.

bitter criticism for a broadcast describing and praising highly Gerson's philosophy and methods of dietary cure. . . . I went to see Gerson. He showed me his records of tumors — even gliomas — apparently cured. But I was still doubtful because it seemed to me inconceivable that anything so serious as a glioma could be cleared up by anything so simple as a diet. He impressed me greatly as a human being, however. This was a man full of idiosyncrasy but also one who knew much, who had suffered much, and who had a sublime faith in his own ideas. . . . At first (Dr. Traeger) violently opposed the Gerson claims, but then he swung over on the ground that, after all, Johnny was deteriorating very fast and in any case the diet could do no harm. . . . We had tried orthodoxy, both static and advanced, and so now we would give heterodoxy a chance. If only we could stave Death off a little longer! And — once more — there was absolutely nothing to lose . . .

"One doctor told us that the reason he had seemed so casual when Johnny entered the Gerson nursing home was his conviction that he couldn't possibly outlast the week anyway . . .

"Within a week, Johnny was feeling, not worse, but much better! The blood count rose steadily . . . the wound in the bulge healed, and miracle of mircles, the bump on the skull was going down! . . .

"I did not know whether or not Gerson could cure, or even check, a malignant glioblastoma. I did learn beyond reasonable doubt that his diet did effect other cures. Gerson himself . . . has never claimed that his diet will 'cure anything,' as his enemies sometimes charge. But some of his results have been astonishing. . . .

"(Dr.) Putman came back from California and paid a call. He was amazed that Johnny was still alive

— let alone that he was well enough to take and pass examinations on schoolwork of the year before. Literally it seemed that Putman could not believe his eyes. . . .

"Since the 'bump' was soft now, the other doctors wanted a minor operation done on Johnny immediately. They felt, at this stage, that drainage might be possible. Dr. Gerson was the lone hold out. The tumor was dead, he insisted, and was working its way out of the boy's head as pus. In addition, anesthesia would be deadly for him."

The argument that followed was a terrible strain on the boy's parents, already near the breaking point from their long and grueling fight. They finally compromised so that Johnny would stay on the Gerson diet and that a freezing agent would be used as an anesthetic.

But Dr. Gerson was right. On the day of the operation, the bump suddenly opened by itself. The surgeon rushed to the boy's room and drained the abscess which extended five centimeters into the brain. A whole cup of pus was taken out!

Johnny's recovery was spectacular. The fearful bump had gone. He laughed often, resumed his studies, and played chess. A miracle had happened!

A few days later the pathologist's report was finished. It showed, as Dr. Gerson had stubbornly insisted, that the discharge was sterile, dead matter. No infection!

And then the eye examination. Pressure from inside the skull against the optic nerve had resulted in a high papilledema, and Johnny's vision had been sharply reduced. Now there was no papilledema, reported the surgeon. The boy's eyes were normal. On top of that, he considered the tumor arrested.

Their joy at hearing this unbelievably good news knew no bounds.

"But there were still plenty of confusions and disappointments too. One doctor would contradict another and then himself — because, in truth, the circumstances were so unprecedented. They were terrifically impressed at what had happened, but they could not explain it or vouch for the future. They soberly could not believe that the Gerson regime alone had produced this effect. But when we asked them 'Would you yourself take the responsibility for taking Johnny *off* that diet, *now?*' they all said, 'No!' "[1]

The following spring, however, Johnny's condition began slowly to worsen. On May 1 he underwent another operation, but the tumor grew back again and it was harder this time. Two months later Johnny succumbed to the enemy he had so valiantly fought.

The loss was a terrible blow to Dr. Gerson. He wrote in *A Cancer Therapy*, "In the development of that therapy 15 years ago, I had several other setbacks; the worst was the loss of 25 patients out of 31 who were just a few months symptom-free and to whom I had administered the opposite sex hormones to give them strength — in accordance with the initial findings of Dr. Charles Higgins. The first five patients felt so much better within a few weeks, and this misled me. This disaster threw me into a deep depression. I almost lost the strength to continue this cancer work, as the worst blow of all was the loss of my young hopeful friend, John Gunther, Jr., who was treated by more than fifteen cancer authorities and given up with a prognosis for a few weeks. However, after a recovery within eight months, I agreed to let him have some sex hormones. Six weeks later the brain tumor regrew,

---

1. op. cit, chap. 3

histologically, an astrocytoma. He was returned to the former treatment and died."

Every scientist, groping for the truth, knows the grim face of failure; and even the prayer that from this death will come many lives does not assuage the lingering sorrow of his loss. For he is, first of all, a human being.

CHAPTER TEN

In answer to an inquiry, the American Medical Association wrote on July 28, 1949: "We have no knowledge of any report published in medical literature describing the medication or the course of treatment sponsored by Gerson, nor do we know of any other investigators who use his methods. Gerson has been invited by this Association to give information on these items, but so far he has never done so."

Perhaps it was this kind of charge that led Dr. Gerson to title Chapter One of his book *A Cancer Therapy*: THE SECRET OF MY TREATMENT — and then open with this wry comment: "Of course, there is none! The heading is used because I am asked frequently, often reproachfully, by physicians about it."

Had normal and accepted channels of publication been open to Dr. Gerson, such confusion might not have existed. Nevertheless, the record is clear on this point. For one who is supposed to have kept his therapy a secret, and despite the fact that "normal" channels were clogged with rejection slips, Dr. Gerson did a pretty good job getting his message across to the people.

The following are some of the articles published by Dr. Max Gerson only since 1941:

"Feeding the German Army," *New York State Journal of Medicine*. 1471.41. 1941.

"Dietary Considerations in Malignant Neoplastic Disease," *Review of Gastroenterology*. Vol. 12, No. 6, pp. 419 to 425 Nov.-Dec. 1945.

"Cancer Research," Hearings before a subcommittee of the United States Senate, S. 1875. July 1, 2, and 3, 1946.

"Effect of a Combined Dietary Regime on Patients with Malignant Tumors," *Experimental Medicine and Surgery*. New York, Vol. VII, Nov. 4, 1949.

"No Cancer in Normal Metabolism," *Medizinische Klinik*,[1] Munich, Jan. 29, 1954, No. 5, pp. 175-179.[2]

"Cancer, a Problem of Metabolism," *Medizinische Klinik*,[1] Munich, June 25, 1954, No. 26.[2]

"Cancer is a Problem of Soil, Nutrition, Metabolism," 1955.

"The Gerson Therapy and Practice in the Prevention of and Treatment for Cancer," 1955.

"Five Case Histories," 1955.

"Rehabilitation of the Cancer Patient," 1956.

"The Problem of Cancer Based upon the Law of Totality," 1956.

"The Historic Development of the Combined Dietary Regime in Cancer," 1956.

"New Therapeutical Approach to Cancer," 1957.

"Cancer — Reflected Symptom of Abnormal Metabolism," *Let's Live*, 1957.[3]

"Can Cancer Be Prevented?" *Prevention Magazine*, 1957.[4]

"A Cancer Therapy — Results of Fifty Cases," *Totality Books*, P.O. Box 1035, Del Mar, CA 92014, 1958.[5]

In addition to these, several articles have been written about Dr. Gerson, describing the theory and diet in detail. Among the more recent:

"This Doctor Cures Cancer!" *Health Saver*, Spring, 1958.

"Dr. Gerson's Cancer Therapy," *Herald of Health*, Oct., 1959, and Nov., 1959.

---

1. Reprinted in the United States.
2. Includes theory and outline of the diet, plus X-rays and case histories.
3. Includes theory and outline of the diet.
4. Includes theory of diet plus case histories.
5. Includes theory, complete diet, plus X-rays and case histories.

It would appear from this partial, but imposing, list that Dr. Gerson's cancer therapy was a secret only to those who didn't know about it.

Does this letter from the Medical Society of the County of New York, May 29, 1953, suggest that Dr. Gerson was reluctant to reveal the details of his treatment:

Dear Dr. Gerson:

We are returning herewith the films and two articles which you so kindly made available to Doctor — —, one of the Censors. Doctor — — wishes me to express his appreciation of your courtesy and frankness in discussing with him your methods of treatment.

> — —, M.D.
> Sincerely yours,
> Chairman, Board of Censors

Or this one of May 3, 1954, by Dr. Gerson:

Doctor — —
Chairman, Special Subcommittee

Medical Society of the County of New York

Dear Doctor — —:

In answer to your letter of April 15, 1954, I am enclosing a photostatic copy of the letter of May 28, 1953, which speaks for itself.

As to the complaints mentioned, of which I would like to have a copy, I wish to say that the records in my office can be looked into by the Committee.

As I have always stated to the medical profession and any investigating body, I am eager to interest them in the results of my cancer treatment, therefore, I highly appreciate your desire to see the real proof, the records and X-rays of these results.

The questions posed in your aforementioned letter are answered in one of my most recent publications, a reprint of which is enclosed. Also enclosed is my treatment book. The treatment I am using is described therein and a more detailed description will be found in a subsequent article now in the process of printing.

I would like to have some assurance that after my presentation before your special subcommittee I will be given an opportunity to make a demonstration of these cases before the entire medical society and that these cases will be published in the New York State Medical Journal. I am obviouly not seeking to suppress it to the attention of the medical profession.

I feel that I am justified by the facts in making these reasonable suggestions as the result of my cases have never been disproven by renowned cancer experts, here and elsewhere. Even after the most searching examinations I have not been successful in having them published in the American medical journals so that they could be brought to the attention and before the scientific critic of the entire profession.

Following is a brief review of my demonstrations:

In July, 1946, by invitation, I demonstrated some cases in Washington, D.C., before the United States Senate subcommittee holding hearings on the Pepper-Neely bill.

In February, 1947, at the request of the Medical Society of the County of New York, I presented fourteen cases before Doctors —— and ——, and about thirty other invited physicians.

Again on invitation I published some articles and demonstrated twenty cases out of forty cases prepared at the Cancer Congress in Berchtesgaden, Germany, October, 1952. Thereafter I was invited to demonstrate a number of cases in the University Clinic in Zurich, Switzerland.

In 1953 I complied with a request of the censors to show films and records to Dr. − −, one of the censors of the County Medical Society. The only tangible result of this cooperation was the letter from Dr. − −, Chairman of the Board of Censors, expressing Dr. − − "appreciation of (my) courtesy and frankness in discussing with him (my) methods of treatment." See enclosed photostat. If desired I will gladly submit a review of the published articles of my cancer work.

In view of the foregoing I feel it not unreasonable to expect that you and your associates on the special subcommittee, after examining and evaluating my cases, should be inclined in the interest of truth and medical progress to recommend that I be granted the opportunity of a demonstration before the whole society and publications in the official journals.

In closing I wish to express my profound gratitude for your reassurance of the complete objectivity of the society and its subcommittee.

Sincerely yours,
MAX GERSON, M.D.

Even when it seemed that Dr. Gerson's patience with the continuing investigations was wearing thin, he remained eminently willing to talk about his work and the details thereof, as witnesses the following interchange of letters with the Medical Society of the County of New York.

Oct. 14, 1954

Dear Dr. Gerson:

The special subcommittee appointed by the Comitia Minora of the Medical Society of the County of N.Y., will meet in room 553 of the Academy of Medicine 2 E. 103rd Street at 8 P.M. on Monday, November 8, 1954, at which time it will be pleased to review with you your clinical records, X-ray pictures, and pertinent data relating to patients with malignant tumors treated by you.

Will you please let me know as soon as possible whether you will be able to attend this meeting.

Sincerely yours,
– –, M.D.
Chairman
Special Subcommittee

On October 25, Dr. Gerson responded:

Dear Dr. – –:

In answer to your letter of Oct. 14. I should like to inform you that this is the fifth invitation to appear before the censors or their subcommittee, where I was informed that physicians and patients complained about my cancer treatment. In my opinion there is one way only to avoid the continued complaints of physicians and their incited patients – that is to arrange that I can publish in our journals and demonstrate my results on patients, most of whom were sent home to die.[1] Deprived of that common right which every physician should have and which the A.M.A. should protect unbiased and especially in such an important medical problem, I again have to request (see my letter of May 3, 1954) that I finally should be granted the right to publish and demonstrate. This right was suppressed since Jan. 8, 1949, when in the *Journal* of the AMA in a critic of several cancer treatments, my treatment was ridiculed and represented among others called "frauds and fables."

---

1. "Ninety to ninety-five per cent of my patients were far advanced (terminal) cases without any risk to take; either all recognized treatments had failed or they were inoperable from the beginning." **Dr. Max Gerson,** *A Cancer Therapy.*

I, on the contrary, presented before and after that critic each time as many patients or more, as I was asked for by the Comitia Minora. Despite the fact that such cancer experts as ——, ——, ——, and others who were officially appointed, could not find any fraud or fable in the results of my treatment, the official representatives of our Medical Association did not even try to make up for the continuation of that injustice.

As a physician of long experience I know that my publications and demonstrations will bring about strict critic and honest endeavor, which will place my treatment where it belongs. Although the new "private" demonstration on Nov. 8 will not clear the situation, I invite the members of the subcommittee to my office a 8 P.M. where I can easier demonstrate some patients with their X-ray and records at that late time, and show as many cases you wish to see. I would prefer, however, if the meeting could be arranged at 5 or 6 P.M.

Enclosed you will find another reprint of a translated article.

Please let me know as soon as possible your friendly answer.

Very sincerely yours,
Max Gerson, M.D.

In addition to Dr. Gerson, the Foundation for Cancer Treatment has been working for years to disseminate information about the doctor's therapy; and like the doctor, this dedicated group has met obstacles every step of the way.

On May 6, 1958, Carl E. Gropler, president of the Foundation, wrote the following letter to *Life* Magazine:

Your article "Fresh Hope on Cancer" in the May 5 issue of *Life* is very well presented and seems quite comprehensive. And yet, to those who have made a more thorough study in this field, it opens a number of questions and leaves them unanswered . . .

"The chemical screening program is inching forward . . ." the article says, but how many years has it been going on and how many millions have been spent?

"There are still only two proved ways — both vastly improved in the last decade — to cure cancer: surgery and radiation . . ." but how long have they been practiced already?

"Victims lose faith in medical help . . ." but when doctors tell the gravely ill or terminal cases, no more can be done by medicine, how can they still retain faith?

And most important of all: "Scientists have shown that the healthy body has a natural resistance to cancer and that greater immunity can be induced." This was first shown by Dr. J. L. Alibert, physician and surgeon at the time of Napoleon, 150 years ago and now again proved in a large experiment. Why has this perception never been pursued more seriously and intensely?

"Further advances depend on radical new approaches . . ." is clearly stated by your article. This most important phase of the cancer problem is conspicuously missing, which makes this excellent news a somewhat one-sided statement far from the usual reporting standard of *Life*.

How about making a real report on this subject?

To present additional, detailed information for your serious consideration, the above-named organization has sent you under separate cover a book just published, written by Max Gerson, M.D.:

A Cancer Therapy — Results of Fifty Cases.

After Dr. Kenneth M. Endicott proudly announces that before long one of the chemotherapists may have *a* cancer patient or *two* cured with drugs, here is a lone physician who without any help is able to present thirty-nine cases "cured" according to the medical definition of the word, the others approaching the five-year mark. Despite the fact that most of them were classified as "terminal cases" they are now leading healthy lives and able to continue their normal activities.

This method and its approach is based on the very fact which the Sloan-Kettering Institute has rechecked so successfully, namely: a healthy body has natural resistance to cancer!

We understand that, during the last ten years, some minor investigations of Dr. Gerson's therapy have been made by medical organizations, but that no statements as to their findings or conclusions were ever released or made available. Dr. Gerson has always been willing and prepared to submit full details about the complete cancer therapy to any and all qualified medical organizations and societies and/or government agencies. Unfortunately, there seems to have been a reluctance to thoroughly check and evaluate this method.

Would you be kind enough to confirm receipt of the above-mentioned book, which we hope will arouse your attention and interest. Should you have any further question or comment to the above, we would appreciate hearing from you and shall be glad to supply any additional information at once.

Yours very truly,

FOUNDATION FOR CANCER TREATMENT, INC.

Carl E. Gropler, President

Naturally, this letter was not printed in *Life*, nor was any suspicion permitted the dignity of print which might suggest that cancer research in America may not be all it could be.

CHAPTER ELEVEN

Wrote Scripps-Howard columnist Ed Koterba on March 4, 1959, concerning the radiation therapy of our late Secretary of State: "I was astounded to learn that the X-ray machine is the same one in use since 1943. In those 16 years, there has been no improvement. It is the same machine which treated, in vain, Sen. Robert Taft.

"Mr. Dulles' treatment has gone on six days a week, since Friday, Feb. 20. The same long trip to the million-volt room."

During this time, public hearings were held by the Senate Committee on Labor and Public Welfare, on the International Health and Medical Research Act of 1959, commonly called the Health for Peace bill. The proposed legislation would authorize an annual appropriation of $50,000,000, in an all-out international effort to fight cancer, heart disease, and other ailments.

I wondered what would come of it. When it is all over and forgotten about, will our medical men still be treating cancer with surgery and radiation? Ten years from today, will there still be telethons and dances and drives to raise money to "fight" cancer?

And will there continue to be little items like this one in your daily newspaper? *"Plunge Kills Patient . . . The body of a cancer patient at —— Hospital was found early today on the roof of the emergency ward seven floors below his room. Police said —— either jumped or fell from a window of his room."*

I suspect there will be, because there is no hope left. Self-delusion may help in its stead, blind faith might carry you through the ordeal, but the intelligent person will always see clearly what the end will be. He will not be deceived, and perhaps that will be the worst for him.

I talked with one of the doctors of the Madison Foundation, which submitted an unfavorable report on Dr. Gerson's therapy. These are his words:

"We reviewed quite a few cases, 20 or 30 maybe, I don't remember. Anyhow we found no evidence that the treatment had any influence. Better forget about a story. That's a very controversial subject and very hot subject with the medical authorities. I would not proceed with anything. Whatever you do, positive or negative, it's still advertising for Gerson, and he gets more pa— I mean, the dumb ones, suckers never die. I mean he has never done anything that was unethical except he's one of those individuals who really believes what he does. He is sincere in his beliefs. He believes in what he says, but he has only one way. He doesn't look to the right and he doesn't look to the left, and no argument can touch him. In my opinion, I would not publish anything, not pro and not con. The guy is obsessed, but he is sincere. He thinks he can do it!"

"Is it possible that he might do some harm with his diet?"

"No. No. That I can sincerely say. He cannot do any harm with the diet. I know his diet too well. The cases I saw of his that came to him in my opinion were all beyond help already when they arrived, all terminal patients, beyond help. Nobody could help. That's why they go to him as a last straw. To his patients — I saw some of his patients — he's Jesus Christ. They believe in him. He is the last word."

"Isn't it possible some of his patients might recover a little bit?"

"Well, there is a certain amount of psychotherapy in all those things, and if you believe in things you feel better. It doesn't last too long in his case, and finally they die; but there is no doubt — and I have seen —

initially they feel better, not that the findings are any different. Those cases I have seen were already beyond help. Most of them had been refused surgical treatment by good institutions like the University of Texas and University of Chicago, and come from all over the globe. The relatives were told that there is nothing they can hope for, and in desperation they turn to Gerson.

"If you want to write your article, write your article. I wouldn't write anything. As far as I'm concerned, I would not subject one of my patients to this treatment. Let them die, but let them die comfortably. If you have cancer that is seated all over, there is nothing you can do about it."

I was thinking of the soldier who suffered from intense headaches and loss of vision and who, after X-rays revealed the presence of a brain tumor, consented to an immediate operation. After the tumor was removed, the soldier improved rapidly; but a few months later began to suffer from worse headaches and loss of vision. Army surgeons wanted to operate again, but he refused. Their warning that he would die did not change his mind, and he was given a medical discharge.

Home in North Bergen, New Jersey, the soldier made the rounds of the doctors. Their answer was the same: "Another operation." In despair, he went to a cancer specialist in New York City and was told that his only chance was surgery.

But on his way home, a friend told him about Dr. Gerson. The soldier went to see him and began the treatment immediately. In a few weeks the headaches stopped and his vision improved. X-rays a few months later showed that the tumor had completely disappeared.

That was in 1944. The soldier is still in perfect

health, is married and is a textile worker in a New Jersey factory.

By word of mouth the story spread quickly through his community, and dozens of people, mostly terminal cases, rushed to the slender, white-haired doctor who believed that "the *results* are decisive," and that "There is no cancer in normal metabolism."

It was results, too, that brought so many patients to Dr. Gerson's door. The soldier's sister-in-law, deeply unhappy that she could not have children, visited a doctor and was told that she had an ovarian tumor which should be operated upon. She went home in tears. With the operation, she would never have children. Without it, she might die.

The soldier sent her to Dr. Gerson, and she began the treatment. Several years later she took her two children to her original doctor. "What a wonderful thing you did," he said. "Since you couldn't have children of your own, adopting these two was a wise move."

"But these are my own children," she said.

The doctor stared at her. "Impossible!"

"I can prove it. Call the Christ Hospital in Jersey City and ask them!"

The doctor did. The hospital confirmed it.

"Our nutrition starts with the soil," said Dr. Gerson. "Man will be forever dependent on the iron laws of nature because the soil produces all his nutrition, as our body is adapted through millions of generations to this natural food. When man disturbs the biological balance there, dire consequences fall on him . . . Rice is the main food staple of Asiatic peoples. When civilization came and polished it to look white and prettier, important minerals and vitamins were removed and thus a disease was caused, called beriberi.

"In addition to damage to the soil, the food is refined, canned, bottled, powdered, frozen, color added, poisoned by sprays, etc., until finally it becomes a mass of dead, unnatural, partly poisoned substances. A body fed in such a way loses the harmony and co-operation of the cells, finally its natural defenses, immunity and healing power.

"That is the reason why our surgeons observe what the statistics show: 'A comprehensive survey of cancer statistics reveals an increase in incidence, morbidity and mortality in spite of improved X-ray techniques, increasingly extensive operative procedures, and education regarding early detection. It appears that the problem of the so-called hopeless case will remain large for some time to come . . .' This is quoted from the *Journal of the American Medical Association*, Vol. 162, No. 8 of October 20, 1956, out of an article by Dr. Bateman.

"Where there is no civilization there is no cancer (the Hunzas, Ethiopian people, etc.) Where civilization starts to change the nutrition, cancer develops.[1]

"It is my conviction that no cancer can develop in a body with normal metabolism. This is the basic fact for the cancer therapy where the liver plays the essential part. The liver is affected to the highest de-

---

1. "I have to point out a happening in the modern civilization of the hospital something which happened on March 27 of this year (1954). On this day we had to perform the first appendicitis operation on a native of this region. How it turned out that this so frequent sickness of white people did not occur in the colored of this country cannot be convincingly explained. Probably its still exceptional occurrence is reducible to a change in the nutrition. Many natives, especially those who are living in large communities do not now live the same way as formerly — they lived almost exclusively on fruits and vegetables, bananas, cassava, ignam, taro, sweet potatoes and other fruits. They now begin to live on condensed milk, canned butter, meat and fish preserves and bread . . . It is obvious to connect the fact of increase of cancer with the increased use of salt by the natives . . ." Dr. Albert Schweitzer, M.D., Lambarene, Africa Hospital·

gree by the artificial, chemical food transformation, as it is the filter for the entire digestive apparatus. It is a storage place and, besides, it transforms the components of our foodstuff. It composes the ingredients for the hormones, activates and reactivates the vitamins and enzymes (there are about 600 different enzymes), thus regulating and protecting the most *vital* process of our life. In addition to these functions, the liver is the most important organ for our detoxication. . . .

"Treating diagnosis is only possible when the localized symptoms, namely the cancer growths, appear. Orthodox medicine is treating these symptoms only. This is apparent by the ever-increasing percentage of recurrencies after the growths are cut out. The real, underlying, cause is neglected. No wonder that many leading surgeons at the ends of their career come to the conclusion that surgery is not the answer to this problem. The same conviction was claimed by the radium and X-ray authorities, who even sent a warning from the International Congress in Rome to the American Medical Association that every X-ray treatment shortened the life of the patient. . . .

"(My) treatment tries to reinstate the natural, normal, biological balance of the body as far as this is possible in the sometimes far-damaged various organs. A restored metabolism helps simultaneously to build up the natural defense, immunity, and healing power of the body.

"The improvement of the metabolism and the liver condition reflects itself immediately — often in days — invisible disappearance of cancers growing on the surface; and this is the best proof of the correctness of this treatment — even in far-advanced, given-up cases. It is deceiving, however, to regard the disappearance of symptoms as a cure. To remove the underlying cause and accomplish the cure of cancer means the re-establishment of the whole metabolism, especially of the liver."

And in another article, Dr. Gerson wrote: "To understand my favorable clinical results by treating the whole metabolism of the cancer patient, I have to go back to the old cancer experiments of Dr. J. L. Alibert, a famous surgeon living in Paris at the time of Napoleon. He was the first who innoculated cancerous material to himself and three of his students. The result was a violent inflammatory reaction lasting a few days, but no cancerous growth appeared in any of the human guinea pigs. These experiments were repeated by Dr. Alibert himself and other colleagues and showed a negative result. The failure to transplant cancer into normal human beings was long regarded, scientifically, as uncertain, as the description of the experiments did not show sufficient scientific accuracy. However, many experiments in the following 150 years did reveal that transplantation of tumors is very difficult, even impossible in healthy animals of the same type, but can be made successful in the animals living under domestic conditions or damaged by abnormal feeding, virus infections or inbreeding, or weakened by inferior inheritance. These conditions increased the susceptibility, but decrease defense and resistance. Therefore, cancer patients often show secondary infections, an abnormal intestinal flora, osteoarthritis, chronic sinus trouble, different types of anemia and other disorders along with the cancer. . . .

"The question of whether cancer can be prevented has to be generally answered as 'no.' To really wipe out cancer, it would be necessary to change our agriculture by avoiding artificial fertilizers and all types of sprays. In addition, it would be necessary to change the ways of preservation and distribution of food and to avoid depriving them of their natural, vital values. That means: not to can, bottle, refine, or subject food to other damaging methods. I think that only some individuals will be able to accomplish the difficult task of avoiding or reducing to a minimum all methods which modern civilization has brought upon us. On the other hand, great revolutionary transformations would be necessary, pressed by the strongest demand of a great part of the population to accomplish this vital task for the well-being of our future offspring.

"As long as all the historical observations and those of our present time remain 'paper warnings' only, we cannot speak about prevention of cancer. Such paper warnings, even given in the strongest and most convincing way did not save old Persia, the ancient Egyptian people, the culture of Greece, and the people of the Roman Empire, (Roma eterna). All these and many more had to go down after 'their modern civilization' ruined the simple habits of life and nutrition, but increased degenerative diseases.

In the United States, our upward rise went quicker than in all other ancient countries and degenerative diseases with cancer and mental sicknesses, have increased much faster too.[1] In the last years degenerative diseases appear in our babies and children, especially in the form of leukemias.[2] It is an illusion that the clinical attempt to detect early symptoms means prevention of cancer. Prevention is possible *only* if we know the cause of cancer. In my opinion it is based upon the degeneration of the liver and I repeat: the

---

1. "In this country more people die of cancer than of any other cause except heart disease. Approximately 1 out of 6 deaths in the United States is caused by cancer . . . It has increased steadily since the turn of the century. In 1900 cancer was in eighth place as a cause of death." The National Cancer Institute.

2. "Cancer is now the leading cause of death among women aged 30-54 and (excluding accidents) among school-age children." *Progress in Health Services,* February 1959, Health Information Foundation, New York.

beginning degenerative changes in the liver do not show any symptoms for a long period.[1] For that reason the removal of one or several cancer symptoms (growths) by operation, or X-ray or radium does not remove the underlying cause, therefore the tumors regrow sooner or later.

"The other question of whether we can cure cancer has been answered in a number of articles that I have published since 1946. I have shown that cancer can be cured even in so-called inoperable or far advanced, given-up cases. . . ."[2]

1. Of 458 Federal employees chosen at random for examinations March 21, 1959, 139 were found to have "potentially cancerous conditions." Report of the N.Y. Cancer Committee. "In a survey of 610 Brooklyn women, designed to uncover hidden cases of cancer, only 207 proved to be free of disease in the pelvic area. More than a third had symptoms suggestive of cancer or a precancerous condition. The results were described by (the) executive vice president of the New York City Cancer Committee as 'shocking.' " — New York Times

2. "Many investigators are not particularly hopeful that a cure for cancer will ever be found, in the sense that penicillin cures many infectious diseases. What they regard as more probable is a chemical control that will prolong useful life by checking the growth and spread of malignant cells, roughly as insulin controls diabetes." *Chemical and Engineering News*, Vol. 33, Page 5138, November 28, 1955, reproduced by U.S. Public Health Service.

CHAPTER TWELVE

I was nearing completion of my story. It was not the one I had gone after, but it was a much greater one. And then one morning as I was going through the newspaper, a line of type leaped up from the obituary page: DR. MAX GERSON, 77, CANCER SPECIALIST. "Dr. Max Gerson, a specialist in the treatment of cancer and tuberculosis, died of pneumonia yesterday in his home. . . ."

I was stunned. I sat in silence for a very long time hardly able to believe or assimilate what I had read. The shock and sense of loss I felt was nearly the same any man would feel when a member of his own family died. It's true I had worked with a reporter's "scientific approach" to the story of Dr. Gerson and cancer. But every reporter knows that a subject of close study, whether he is a best friend or very worst foe, becomes a part of the author. Thus when death comes, it is also something personal that departs.

But deeper than my own feeling for myself was the terrible knowledge that Dr. Max Gerson's fight was finished. I thought of all those in the future who would need his help but would never have it. Heartsick, I tried to think of all the good he had done and the many people he had helped. I remembered the case of the woman crippled by arthritis for so many years, semi-paralyzed, who had been brought to Dr. Gerson after the long orthodox treatments had failed. Within three weeks she was able to move her toes and fingers. Later, she returned to the clinic in Baltimore and told her doctor what had happened. "I suppose you disapprove," she said.

His answer was startling. "Not only do I not disapprove, but I am not surprised at the results. That man will probably not live to see it, but they will be erecting monuments to him. At the moment, however, he is a thorn in their side."

I remembered the last time I had seen Dr. Gerson, and how that dedicated little group, The Foundation for Cancer Treatment, heard Dr. Gerson, with tears in his eyes, tell of the death of one of his patients. She had been under treatment for six months and was in good condition. After the breakup of her marriage she had discontinued the treatments.

During that meeting, too, Dr. Gerson discussed the Long John radio program and his subsequent suspension. His appearance had been hastily arranged, he said, and no thought had been given to possible consequences. Apparently the Board of Censors of the New York Medical Society construed his appearance as personal advertising for him. He replied that he did not need to advertise for patients, as he had more than he could handle. They asked him where he got all his patients. Dr. Gerson replied: "First they go to you, then to an osteopath, then to a chiropractor, and then they come to me. *Why don't you cure them?*"

I learned that there were nurses in major hospitals who knew of Dr. Gerson and would quietly suggest to incurable patients that they go to him. When one such patient came to Dr. Gerson, he sent an authorization to the hospital for her medical report.

"After they sent me the report," Dr. Gerson said, "physicians called, nurses called her every day: 'We'd like to see you, re-examine you, like to do this, like to do that.' She refused, 'I feel better, I feel excellent. I will not go. You told me you could not help me any more: Please let me alone!' But they don't."

Dr. Gerson was excited during the meeting. He had developed a technique that was successful even on patients who had undergone previous cobalt treatments.

"I never had results with cobalt treatments," he said, "but despite this, it worked! Now we see the most wonderful results of our life. I have now an esophagus cure, the first in the annals of medicine."

The cancer had localized on the fifth vertebra of the patient, near the heart, and was inoperable. It became impossible for him to eat, and then to drink. Eventually he could hardly breathe. After the futile cobalt treatments, he was brought to Dr. Gerson. Eight days later he could swallow, eat, and drink. Unbelievably, he returned to work as an auto mechanic.

"The doctor had told him he would have to have a tube in his stomach to take food," said Dr. Gerson gleefully. "Now his only complaint, every two hours the enema!"

And I remember the statement at the Senate hearings: "It would be a calamity if anything happened to Dr. Gerson with no one left to carry on in this particular field. . . . "

When, I wondered, would they start building the monuments?

The news of Dr. Gerson's passing was cabled to Dr. Albert Schweitzer at his hospital in Lambarene, Gabon, French Equatorial Africa. His moving letter to Mrs. Gerson is a monument in itself to the memory of his dear friend.

(Translation of a letter from Dr. Albert Schweitzer)

Lambarene, Gabon, French Equatorial Africa
Dear Mrs. Gerson: March 10, 1959
A little while ago your husband wrote me that he would like to see me again and that I should let him know when I would be in Europe. Gladly I made a note of this, for I, too, had the desire to sit down again with him quietly . . . And now he has passed away!

I was moved that you sent me a cable as if I belonged to the family. How I take part in the loss you suffer you know; and that I mourn a friend in the departed, whom I counted among my closest, you also know. I owe him such gratitude for all that he did for my wife. Without him she would have died when our child was small. How gratefully she always thought of him!

But in the hour when I received the news of his death, I also thought about what he has meant to the world. I see in him one of the most eminent medical geniuses in the history of medicine. He possessed something elemental. Out of deepest thought about the nature of disease and the process of healing, he came to walk along new paths with great success. Unfortunately, he could not engage in scientific research or teach; and he was greatly impeded by adverse political conditions. In ordinary times he would have been able to expound his ideas for many years as professor at one of the important German universities; would have taught pupils who could carry on his research and teachings; would have found recognition and encouragement . . . All this was denied him.

His was the hard lot of searching and working as an uprooted immigrant, to be challenged and to stand as a fighter. We who knew and understood him admired him for working his way out of discouragement again and again, and for undertaking to conquer the obstacles.

Many of his basic ideas have been adpated without having his name connected with them. Yet he has achieved more than seemed possible under these adverse circumstances. He leaves a legacy which commands attention and which will assure him his due place. Those he cured will now attest to the truth of his ideas. I hope that he also gained some pupils in the new world who will do this for him.

We who knew and valued him mourn him already today as a medical genius who walked among us and as a man who was destined to be a fighter who proved himself in this adverse fate.

With loving thoughts, your devoted

ALBERT SCHWEITZER

CHAPTER THIRTEEN

While writing the story of Dr. Gerson, I couldn't help feeling it was too shocking to believe. The friends with whom I discussed it became almost angry in their denial that anything of the sort could happen in this day and age. It developed that we were all naive. There is plenty of controversy about cancer; there are a number of independent little groups across the nation fighting their own one-sided battles; there had been dozens of lone scientists with exciting cancer treatments who had been stamped out of existence and driven to spending their last days in solitude and bitterness.[1]

But the public at large, deafened by a barrage of fearful warnings and publicity from the vested interests of medicine, never hears their cries — or scoffs at their presumption.

In the Congressional Record, I came across the Krebiozen scandal. On August 23, 1958, the Hon. Roland V. Libonati of Illinois made these remarks in the House of Representatives: "Mr. Speaker, the story of Krebiozen is a sad one, and by their unfounded opposition, several past officials of the American Medical Association have been guilty of heinous actions against a great scientist in the medical profession, Dr. Andrew C. Ivy, who presently holds the high position of distinguished professor of physiology and head of the Department of Clinical Science of the University of Illinois, as well as his membership in the Chicago Medical Society.

"A true scientist is a man who seeks the truth, and Dr. Andrew C. Ivy exemplifies that type of man. In his experimentations with 250 other physicians, all

---

1. Natenberg, Maurice: *The Cancer Blackout,* Chicago: Regent House, 1959.

members of the AMA, he has proved that there is biological activity in the use of this drug.

"Dr. Stevan Durovic and his brother, Marko Durovic, have spent large sums of their own and their friends' money in Argentina in the development of the discovery of Krebiozen as well as thousands of dollars to the Krebiozen Foundation, to place the drug at the disposal of cancer victims, terminal cases, who were doomed to die.

"Personally, I am well acquainted with the whole story in view of the fact that I acted as vice chairman of the committee and the commission, duly appointed by the Illinois Legislature, to conduct an inquiry to determine whether or not there was a conspiracy to prevent freedom of research at the University of Illinois, a tax-supported institution. A great deal of testimony given by many expert witnesses at those hearings proved beyond a doubt that false reports were released to the public by medical stooges of the AMA to destroy public confidence in the scientific findings conducted by Dr. Ivy and his fellow medics. This subject was in controversy for a period of five years, and still continues today in spite of the reports that have been released showing favorable results made by those individual doctors on their own cases. . .

"The subject matter and testimony, together with conclusions thereon, were masterfully presented in the two books written by Mr. Herbert Baily, *K-Krebiozen, Key to Cancer?* published in 1955, and *A Matter of Life or Death* recently published by G. P. Putnam's Sons, a concern that is very selective on printing any books, and especially those touching on scientific subjects, as to their value and veracity. . . .

". . . Unless something is done to remedy the present unfortunate standoff situation preventing an authentic test of Krebiozen, I will proceed in the 86th Congress, God granting my presence, to introduce a resolution to investigate those elements that are preventing the carrying out of such a test, on the grounds that the public interest demand such action. It is fundamental that a conspiracy to prevent scientific research is in itself within the congressional prerogative to protect the welfare of the people of the United States.

"No organization can defy or deny the right of justice to be meted out to honest men and their works, especially in this case, directly affecting thousands of unfortunates, who die every year with great suffering and at great cost to their families, or the charitable institutions which are established throughout the land for this cause.

"I am warning the American Medical Association at this time, as I did before in the Illinois State Assembly, to pay heed to Dr. Ivy's appeal for fair play and give Dr. Andrew C. Ivy a fair chance to prove what he contends is of benefit to mankind."

On February 12, 1959, I found these remarks by Mr. Libonati in the Congressional Record: "Mr. Speaker, the Krebiozen controversy remains at the 'do nothing yet' dead center stage; its test committee conferences never seem to reach a true solution as to the selection of an honest method to be used to scientifically test the drug in its reaction on the cancer patient.

"Meanwhile, thousands die of the malady and other thousands suffer the poisoning agonies of the putrefaction of live body tissues of the victim approaching death. No one seems to care. Certainly, no one in the million dollar fund-raising cancer clinics are excited over the almost miraculous nine-year record of the Krebiozen Research Foundation's medical records; and reports of the 500 doctors who used Krebiozen in the treatment of cancer patients, all terminal cases. Yes, other doctors told loved ones, 'It is hopeless, the patient will die shortly, nothing can be done. It's only a matter of time.'

"But there are real God-fearing men in the medical profession who love humanity and life by the sacred oath of Hippocrates.

"They used Krebiozen, some secretly, in order to escape the vicious opposition of their fellows, and these kept a steady vigil over the sick, registering every change in the patient. These records are the undeniable testimonials to the scientific value of Krebiozen in cancer study:

"First. Krebiozen relieved pain when sedatives failed.

"Second. Krebiozen reduced the size of the carcinoma in certain types of cancer cases.

"Third. Krebiozen stimulated the appetite of the patient to partake of food, thus gaining natural strength.

"Fourth. It caused bed patients, eight months abed, to leave their beds and become ambulatory.

"Fifth. Krebiozen is biologically active.

"Sixth. Krebiozen is the key to the arrestment and control of cancer.

"Seven. Krebiozen is one of the answers to a study of new scientific areas and methods in the fight on cancer which will ultimately result in a cure for cancer."

On February 16, 1959, Mr. Libonati continued his battle in the Krebiozen controversy by quoting a letter he had written to an attorney, who had congratulated him on his efforts. The letter read in part: ". . . There is no question but that the American Cancer Society is dominated by the American Medical Association, and the evasive answers to your questions only proved that the board of directors and the various committees which passed upon this request, with their 'do nothing' policy, is a result of this vicious pressure. . . .

"Maybe the raising of millions of dollars of funds for charitable projects has become a 'racket,' and the longer that they remain in the test-tube stage of development, the longer patronage and job payrollers remain in their soft berths.

"Would you please be so kind as to indicate to me your attitude in this matter, as it is important that we trace the malignant job-growth of this charity to its source. They quibble too much over procedures for their honesty of purposes while we seek a cure. They complain too loudly against another who, seemingly, has perfected a work that the public expects its charity dollars to do. Maybe we should investigate the American Cancer Society's operations. At least their 'do nothing' attitude creates a suspicion that they don't want a cure or that their desire is to prolong the agony of others, while they fiddle around, trying to perfect their own cure. Some progress should have been made up to this time in the control of cancer by them. Krebiozen has a record that anyone can read in the reports of the Krebiozen Research Foundation, given by 500 doctors in actual cases which they have treated. . ."

And on March 3, 1959, Mr. Libonati said this in the House of Representatives: "Mr. Speaker, I attended a testimonial dinner in honor of Dr. Andrew Conway Ivy, the champion of the scientific doctrine of freedom of research, which has suffered in recent years through the falsity of certain politico-physician leaders of the American Medical Association, who faked reports, suppressed honest information, brutally slugged the opposition, both physically and through pressures, used to prevent the truth about Krebiozen reaching the American people."

Strong words, these, from an elected representative of the people. Alarming words. Because the Krebiozen controversy was allied to my own story, I managed to get hold of a copy of Herbert Bailey's book, *A Matter of Life or Death*. It was shocking, and I strongly advise anyone who is interested in the subject to obtain either or both of the two books mentioned by Mr. Libonati. From there, he can make up his own mind, but it is senseless to argue the point emotionally without knowing the facts, or knowing only the claims made by a single side.

I do not want to tell the story of Krebiozen. It has already been told, and is still being told by others. My point in bringing it up stems from the skepitcal ears. Mine were skeptical, too, before I satisfied myself with the facts.

I called Mr. Bailey and asked him what it would take to have Krebiozen recognized.

"I think there would have to be a Congressional investigation of the AMA, and I don't think that's too far off," he said. "If we win this thing, there's going to be an investigation. And now, actually, Dr. Ivy has 50 cases which have been cancer-free five years or more.[1] He presented these at the testimonial dinner about three weeks ago in Chicago. They carried banner headlines in Chicago, and papers across the country ran it, but only one New York paper picked it up. At any rate, with that kind of evidence — and the evidence grows every day — eventually the pressure will be too great, public opinion too strong, and the opposition of the AMA will be eliminated.

"I think fully half of all doctors would like to see this happen. A great many doctors support the AMA, but not half so many as they would have you believe. I mean by that they are on the side of organized medicine, but are not devoted followers of the AMA because they have to live in fear of it. They would prefer an organization that would be less clouting them on the head all the time.

"Mainly, doctors are ignorant of the true story of

1. The latest figure is reportedly 150 patients who have been cancer-free from four to ten years.

Krebiozen. Once they read my book — and this has been shown many times — they are convinced.

"I'm expecting this thing to break wide open in the near future. The Committee for a Fair Test of Krebiozen at 343 S. Dearborn Street in Chicago has been fighting long and hard for a fair test of this drug, and I believe they are going to get it."

I asked Herbert Bailey if he knew of Dr. Gerson's work.

"I met him, you know, and I thought a lot of his treatment, really. I didn't know too much about his treatment, but I did go around several months ago and saw some of the records of his cases. I was very favorably impressed by what I saw. Certainly the theory is very good, and the fact that he had terminal cases is very impressive. A man like Albert Schweitzer certainly wouldn't support Gerson if he didn't have something.

"It stands to reason there's something to it. Now Gerson had five committees to investigate him, and they came, were satisfied, and left — and nothing came of it. Of course, Dr. Lincoln up in Massachusetts went through the same thing. Well, it killed him. And I think he's got something, too. He used the bacteria phage method very successfully. They've been more or less swept out of the cancer field by the powers that be, but they're having very good success with other diseases. And it's got a very fine rationale. I would say there are at least a dozen such therapies which have shown promise on patients.

"I've seen these things happen first hand with Krebiozen, and I have correspondence with many others. I know they've been persecuted and hounded practically out of existence.

"By the way, I know of a doctor who is using both the Gerson method and Krebiozen conjointly, and I think it works better that way. This doctor has had a very great success with it. You're getting the diet, and then you're getting the natural body hormone which the body does not have in sufficient quantity. I am sure that eventually Gerson will come into his own."

But Dr. Gerson would never see that day. He had left his legacy. It was up to others to use it wisely . . . or to bury it with him.

CHAPTER FOURTEEN

Dr. Gerson's work was not buried with him. *Mrs. Charlotte R. Straus, whose address is Post Office Box 1035, Del Mar, California 92014,* still carries on educational work and some M.D.'s are using the Gerson treatment. Others, who believe in it, do not care to take the professional risks involved in using it in their practice. Many pressures can be brought to bear on them to dissuade them — especially if they work in a hospital. This happened during Dr. Gerson's lifetime, to the radiologist at a N.Y. hospital who was furnishing him with X-rays. He was made to stop. It happened more recently, in 1962, to a doctor who was using the Gerson therapy in a New Jersey clinic. He was made to close his doors and is at this writing, attempting to get permission to use the Gerson therapy experimentally.

What Albert Schweitzer wrote of Dr. Gerson — "Many of his basic ideas have been adapted without having his name connected with them" — is becoming more undeniable every day. The intransigent, self-serving close-mindedness of some members of organized medicine is being shattered by sharp truths fired by scientists from all over the country.

It is becoming embarrassingly clear to the big "cancer research" organizations, that no matter how many guinea pig volunteers at U.S. penitentiaries they innoculate with live cancer cells, the subjects do not get cancer. No matter how much time is wasted repeating this experiment and how much public money is spent in a benighted effort to square a circle, the luster of Dr. Gerson's words, "There is no cancer in normal metabolism," grows brighter.

This viewpoint is no longer as controversial as it once was. Today, a doctor from the Mayo Clinic and Mayo Foundation can tell the board of trustees of the

Allergy Foundation that allergy is believed to be closely related to the natural processes of immunity, which include the body's production of antibodies to combat invasion by germs, and that evidence of many kinds has shown that factors in the body's resistance are associated closely with the inception and subsequent course of human cancer. Theorists have suggested, reported the doctor, that cancer cells may develop from time to time in the normal body, but that most of these are sufficiently abnormal to be attacked successfully by the body's natural defenses.

Today, it is becoming increasingly difficult to deny the role of the liver in cancer, as Dr. Gerson stressed above all in his therapy, especially since the discovery of the TIP — Tumor Inhibitory Principle — which is manufactured by this organ. "The normal liver," reported the *New York Times* of June 30, 1961, "produces a chemical factor that powerfully inhibits growth of experimental cancer in mice, a specialist reported here yesterday.

"The factor is imparted both to the blood serum and to the bile, according to the report. It has not been found in cancer patients.

". . . the evidence suggests the hypothesis that deficiency, either hereditary or acquired, of such inhibitory factors might be fundamental to the cause of cancer."

Today, it is becoming increasingly difficult to ridicule the role of nutrition in cancer, especially since a recognized investigator discovered that a radical change in the diet of trout from scraps of meat to pieces of bread ruined their livers and caused a plague of cancer among them.

It is also becoming increasingly difficult to deny the connection between cancer and "civilized" eating, when so many previously cancer-free societies, including the Eskimos, are seeing their first cases of cancer among their people when the white men come, bringing with them the "benefits" of civilization.

However, it is still not difficult to deny that any important inroads have been made in the fight against cancer. A 1957 survey by the Society of Actuaries of more than 100,000 group surgical insurance claims disclosed that one out of every seven operations was for cancer. The figure for the 1947 study — same number of claims — revealed that cancer surgery was responsible for only one out of every fourteen. The Health Insurance Institute, which made this report, represents the Health Insurance Association of America, which has more than 250 insurance companies as members.

Have you read anything in the U.S. press about the most sensational medical trial in recent history, the trial of Dr. Joseph Issels in Munich, Germany, in the summer of 1961? You haven't seen a word about it? Strange, because nearly every newspaper, tabloid and magazine in all Europe and in many other countries of the world covered it fully; and *Der Spiegel* — the German equivalent of our *Time* magazine — gave it an unheard-of 12 pages, with Dr. Issels' picture on the cover.

The issue in this trial was: "Can a doctor explore new ways of treatment of terminal cancer patients other than those prescribed by orthodox medicine?"

On trial was Dr. Joseph Issels, who, in 1951, opened the First National Clinic for Internal Treatment of Cancer in Rottach-Egern on the Tegernsee. Many details and aspects of his treatment were very similar to the therapy of Dr. Gerson.

In 1951 a Medical Totality Congress (doctors who believe in treating the whole person, not just a part of him) met in Berchtesgaden, Germany. Dr. Gerson was invited to give a lecture before these eminent physicians. His speech was scheduled for an afternoon session, but by unanimous acclamation, was continued long into the evening hours.

Dr. Gerson presented his own concept of the origin of cancer, believing it to arise from an underlying, general disorder caused by inherited or acquired defects and nutritional deficiences. Since orthodox medicine holds cancer to be a local disease, local treatment is therefore emphasized; operation and radiation with some chemotherapy added and though their techniques have greatly improved, the percentage of failures seems to increase as the underlying conditions continue to produce new growths.

Dr. Gerson explained how he based his theory and practice on the principle that a healthy body does not produce cancer but can even fight it off. In his practice of 95% terminal cases, Dr. Gerson described how he developed and applied his treatment. It has for its main purpose the restoration of body functions, if still possible, sufficiently for the body to eliminate its toxins and poisons and reinstate the body chemistry necessary to maintain health.

A question-and-answer period followed. Dr. Gerson described his method and its practical management, namely raw and freshly cooked fruits and vegetables, large amounts of various specific juices freshly pressed several times daily, emphatic elimination measures with frequent enemas, liver therapy with injections of calf's liver juices as well as medication individually adapted by the doctor, consisting mainly of vitamins and minerals, and after a few weeks some light proteins such as yogurt, cottage cheese, etc.

One of the participants at this congress, Dr. Joseph Issels, reportedly showed burning interest in this treatment, and sat down with Dr. Gerson after the lecture for several hours to ask innumerable questions and take detailed notes.

The volume in Dr. Issels' clinic grew steadily.

Among 95% terminal cases he could unquestionably show unusual, positive results. On September 15 ,1960, he was arrested for fraud and manslaughter; fraud, because he was said to have promised cures to terminal patients and their families; manslaughter, because the district attorney was able to produce three cases of patients who died, but who might have lived longer, he averred, if all orthodox methods had been used before or instead of the Issels treatment.

One of the most respected medical experts in Europe, Professor Dr. Schulten, asserted that only a world medical congress could render final judgment about the effectiveness of Issels' methods. The presiding judge therefore barred any evidence concerning the value of the Issels method, and in forbidding this discussion, the court denied it an airing before the public. Other startling evidence, however, was revealed with the testimony that a dentist formerly on the staff at the clinic had been paid $2,500 by a certain medical organization to collect material which could prove damaging to Dr. Issels, and which was eventually used in the trial.

In his defense, Dr. Issels charged that the accusation was based on the latest knowledge of medical science which still concedes ignorance about the real cause and final cure of cancer. But in its fight against this enigma, he said, the orthodox school used operation, radiation, and certain chemotherapy which proved only partially effective but are known at the same time carcinogenous.[1] No one wishes to question this contradiction, but he, Issels, is being tried for treating mostly terminal patients with harmless means

1. "Thyroid cancer is increasing among young children, apparently as a result of radiation treatments for other ailments around the head and neck, according to Dr George Crile, Jr., head of the department of surgery, Cleveland Clinic Foundation." — News item, *N.Y. World-Telegram.*

which had all been used on himself and his family as well.

Charges for fraud were dropped, but Dr. Issels received a one-year suspended sentence for manslaughter, which he appealed immediately. The last word in this trial is surely yet to be heard, especially since one of the prosecution's witnesses was recently proved to have committed perjury.

Editorials and reader's comments in the German press were almost unanimous in their condemnation of the presumption that a court of law could assume jurisdiction over an area of science which had not yet yielded up its ultimate secrets and for which millions are being spent by governments and public donations every year.

Only 18% of X-ray therapy and surgery is successful, one newspaper thundered, and yet authorities keep asking us to get our checkups and X-rays. For what? Is this at all a trial? What has this doctor done? Especially since he only *adds* his therapy, to cure the incurable, to the orthodox methods. Is it necessary to have such trials at all?

Concluded *Der Spiegel*: "It is practically impossible to say who is right and who is wrong. Nobody comes out either clean or dirty. Nobody really knows what cancer is."

"Maybe in one to three years we might know," said radiologists and surgeons from famous clinics in Germany and Austria.

Asked the D.A. at the trial: "Know what?"

"Which treatment is effective against cancer."

The history of medicine is a story of almost incredible stupidity, and a story of almost incredible genius and perseverance. Nearly every single advance, nearly every single discovery, has met with such furious opposition by the medical fraternity that one wonders how medicine has advanced at all. Years, decades, sometimes centuries were allowed to elapse between discovery and approval, and millions of lives were lost because of it. Medical pioneers have been imprisoned, executed, hounded, and driven insane for their genius. Their names are now the names of heroes, and every schoolboy knows them.

Does Dr. Gerson's name belong on the list?

Tomorrow, will the world say of him, "He was a fool who offered hope where there was no hope, and life when there was no life to give?"

Or will they say: "He could look at the evidence planted in the universe and from it derive a new concept, and a greater thing than this no mind can accomplish."

DIRECTIONS FOR GENERAL NUTRITION[1]

". . . . The way in which the fundamentals are described here is derived from many long years of experience with people rejected from military service or denied life insurance.

"They were made acceptable by following these directions. Thousands of patients were given this advice after their recovery from chronic sicknesses, and most of them included their families in this pattern of nutrition for many years. The results were satisfactory. The majority remained in good health, were acceptable for life insurance and other services and increased their strength and working power. My family and I too, have followed these directions for more than thirty years.

"The outline permits sufficient margin for personal living habits, family feasts and holidays, as one quarter of all of the food should be to one's choice; the remainder should be taken for the purpose of protecting the functions of the highly essential organs — liver,

---

1. From A Cancer Therapy, by Max Gerson, M.D.

kidneys, brain, heart, etc. — by storing reserves and avoiding an unnecessary burden on these vital organs. To save our body from extra work in the disposal of excessive food, especially fats which are difficult to digest, the destruction of poisons, etc., is a precaution that may prevent many kinds of acute and chronic sickness in organs somewhat weaker in origin and development or previously damaged. That this outline is written to prevent sickness, not to cure it, must be stressed beforehand. The purpose of healing demands a much deeper dietetic encroachment and a medication directed to the pathology of the body's chemistry after a diagnosis is established.

". . . As science is not yet developed to the point of knowing all the enzymes, vitamins and many biological functions of hormones and minerals, it is safer to use foods in the most natural form, combined and mixed by nature and raised, *if possible,* by an organic gardening process, thus obeying the laws of nature. This observation helped the human race for thousands of years before any science was developed. In this way we bring in all known vitamins and enzymes, both the discovered and the undiscovered ones, and especially the unknown, to quote Professor Kollath, 'life stimulating substances,' given best as fresh as possible and not damaged by refining or preserving processes, such as canned food. These contain all of the necessary substances in their proper quantity, mixture and composition, and are regulated by instinct, hunger, taste, smell, sight and other factors.

"Three quarters of the food which should be consumed include the following:

"All kinds of fruits, mostly fresh and some prepared in different ways; freshly prepared fruit juices (orange, grapefruit, grape, etc.); fruit salads; cold fruit cups; mashed bananas, raw, grated apples, applesauce, etc.

"All vegetables freshly prepared, some stewed in their

own juices and others either raw or finely grated, such as carrots, cauliflower or celery; vegetable salads, soups, etc.; some dried fruits and vegetables are permitted but not frozen ones.

"Potatoes are best when baked; the contents may be mashed with milk or soup; they should seldom be fried and preferably boiled in their jackets.

"Salads of green leaves or mixed with tomatoes, fruits, vegetables, etc.

"Bread may contain whole rye or wheat flour, or these may be mixed; it should be refined as little as possible. Oatmeal should be used freely. Buckwheat cakes and potato pancakes are optional, as are brown sugar, honey, maple sugar and maple candy.

"Milk and milk products, such as pot cheese and other kinds of cheese which are not greatly salted or spiced, buttermilk, yogurt and butter. Cream and ice cream should be reduced to *a minimum* or restricted to holidays (ice cream is 'poison' for children).

"The remaining one-fourth of the dietary regime which allows for personal choice, may consist of meat, fish, eggs, nuts, candies, cakes or whatever one likes best. Nicotine should be avoided; liquors, wines and beer should be reduced to a minimum in favor of fresh fruit juices; coffee and tea should be cut to minimum with the exception of the following teas; peppermint, chamomile, linden flower, orange flower, and a few others.

"Salt, bicarbonate of soda, smoked fish and sausage should be avoided as much as possible, as should sharp condiments such as pepper and ginger, but fresh garden herbs should be used — onions, parsley leaves, chives, celery and even some horseradish.

"As for vegetables and fruits, they should, I repeat, be stewed in their own juices to avoid the loss of minerals easily dissolved in water during cooking. It seems that these valuable minerals are not so well absorbed when they are out of their colloidal state.

"All vegetables may be used. Especially recommended for their mineral content are carrots, peas, tomatoes, Swiss chard, spinach, string beans, Brussels sprouts, artichokes, beets cooked with apples, raisins, etc.

"The best way to prepare vegetables is to cook them slowly for one and one-half to two hours, without water. To prevent burning, place an asbestos mat under the saucepan. You may also use some stock of soup or else sliced tomatoes may be added to the vegetables. This also will improve the taste. Spinach water is too bitter for use; it generally is not liked and should be drained off. Onions, leeks and tomatoes have enough liquid of their own to keep them moist while cooking. (Beets should be cooked like potatoes, in their jackets and with water.) Wash and scrub vegetables thoroughly, but do not peel or scrape them. Saucepans must be tightly covered to prevent steam from escaping. Covers must be heavy or close fitting. Cooked vegetables may be kept in the refrigerator overnight. To warm them, heat slowly with a little soup or fresh tomato juice."

Translation of the Titles of Scientific Works
by
Max Gerson, M.D.

1907. Dissertation Article: Influence of the Artificial Hyperemia and Blood Transfusions in the Treatment of Fractures in the Hip Joint.

1910. Bromocol Poisoning. Aerztliche Sachverstaendigen-Zeitung.

1916. Myasthenic Bulbar Paralysis - Berliner Klinische Wochenschr. No. 51.

1918. Reflex Hyperesthesia. Zeitschrift fuer die gesamte Neurologie und Psychiatrie.

1919. Paralysis Found in Diphtheria Carriers. Berliner Klinische Wochenschrift, No. 12.

1921. Concerning the Etiology of Multiple Sclerosis. Deutsche Zeitschrift fuer Nervenheilkunde.

1924. Constitutional Basis for Nervous Symptoms. Fortschritte der Medizin, No. 1. P. 9.

1926. Experiments Attempting to Influence Severe Forms of Tuberculosis Through Dietetic Treatment. Muenchener Medizinische Wochenschrift, No. 2 and 3.

1929. Origin and Development of the Dietetic Treatment of Tuberculosis. Die Medizinische Welt 1929, No. 37.

1929. Treatment of Rickets and Tuberculosis. Deutsche Medizinische Wochenschrift 1929. No. 38.

1930. Several Experiments with the Gerson Diet in Tuberculosis. Medizinische Welt 1930.

1930. Salt Association with Migraine (An early factor in dietetic treatment. Verhandlungen der Deutschen Gesellschaft fuer Innere Medizin 1930. P. 129. No. 23.

1930. Basic approaches to the Gerson Diet. Muenchener Medizinische Wochenschrift No. 23, P. 967.

1930. Phosphorus, Cod Liver Oil and the Gerson Diet in the Treatment of Tuberculosis. Deutsche Medizinsche Wochenschrift No. 12.

1930. Several Factors in Dietetic Treatment of Pulmonary Tuberculosis. Zeitschrift fuer Aerztliche Fortbildung. No. 11.

1931. Nicotine as a Deterrent Factor in the Treatment of Lupus. Verhandlungen der Deutschen Gesellschaft Fuer Innere Medizin.

1931. Several Experiments in the Dietary Treatment of Tuberculosis. Verhandlungen der Deutschen Gesellschaft fuer Innere Medizin.

1931. Resume of Varying Sensory Factors in the Treatment of Lupus. Verhandlungen der Deutschen Gesellschaft fuer Innere Medizin.

1931. Basis Underlying Discontinuance of Salt Free Diet in Tuberculosis Sanitariums. Deutsche Medizinische Wochenschrift, 1931. No. 8.

1931. The Dietetic Problems of the Present Day in the Treatment of Tuberculosis. The Journal of State Medicine Vo.. XXXLX No. 8 London.

1931. Sedimentation in the Dietetic Treatment of Lung Tuberculosis. Zeitschrift fuer Tuberculose 1932. Bd. 63 Heft 5.

1932. The Gerson Diet in Chronic Pulmonary Spastic Diseases and Hypertension. Wiener Klinische Wochenschrift 1932. No. 13.

1932. Observations on the Gerson Diet. Wiener Klinische Wochenschrift No. 37. 1932.

1932. The Gerson Diet in Practice - Technisch - Pharmazeutische Aerztezeitung. Wein 1932. No. 20.

1932. Dietary Treatment of Migraine and Pulmonary Tuberculosis. Wiener Klinische Wochenschrift 1932. No. 24.

1932. Gerson Diet on Pulmonary Tuberculosis and Migraine. Mitteilungen des Volksgesundheitsamtes. Jahrgang 1932. Wien, Heft 9.

1934. Psychic Reactions During the Gerson Diet in Pulmonary Tuberculosis. Phychotherapeutische Praxis. Vol. 1, Heft 4, 1934.

1935. High Fluid and Potassium Diet as Treatment in Cardiorenal Insufficiene. Muenchener Medizinische Wochenschrift No. 15.

1935. Feeding of the Tubercular. Wiener Klinische Wochenschrift No. 9.

1935. Non-Specific Desensitations by Means of Diet in Allergic Skin Diseases. Dermatologische Wochenschrift 1935. No. 15.

1935. The Recession of Inflammation in Gerson Diet with Special Reference to Tubercular Inflammations. Wiener Klinische Wochenschrift 1935. No. 25.

1935. The Administration of Liver Extract in Relation to Diet in the Treatment of Chronic Diseases. Wiener Medizinische Wochenschrift 1935. No. 40.

1935. The Gerson Diet in Home Practice. Der Oesterreichische Arzt. Folge 2, Jahrgang 2.

1941. Feeding the German Army. New York State Journal of Medicine. 1471. 41 1941.

1943. Some Aspects of the Problem of Fatigue. The Medical Record, New York. June 1943.

1945. Dietary Considerations in Malignant Neoplastic Disease. Review of Gastroenterology. Vol. 12, No. 6, Pages 419 to 425. Nov. - Dec. 1945.

1948. The Significance of the Content of Soil to Human Disease.

1949. Effect of a Combined Dietary Regime on Patients with Malignant Tumors. Experimental Medicine and Surgery. New York Vol. VII, Nov. 4, 1949.

1954. No Cancer in Normal Metabolism. Medizinische Klinik, Munich. Jan. 29. 1954, No. 5, page 175-179.

1954. Cancer a Problem of Metabolism. Medizinische Klinik, Munich. No. 26, June 25, 1954.

1955. Cancer is a Problem of Soil, Nutrition, Metabolism.

1955. Are Soil, Food and Metabolic Disturbances Basically Responsible for Cancer Development?

1955. The Gerson Therapy and Practice in the Prevention of and Treatment for Cancer.

1955. Five Case Histories.

1952. Cancer Development and Treatment. Lecture at the Academy of Applied Nutrition (Pasadena).

1956. Rehabilitation of the Cancer Patient.

1956. The Problem of Cancer Based upon the Law of Totality.

1956. The Historic Development of the Combined Dietary Regime in Cancer.

1957. Can Cancer be Prevented? Prevention Magazine.

1957. New Therapeutical Approach to Cancer.

1957. Cancer — Reflected Symptoms of Abnormal Metabolism.

Books

1930. My Diet. - Edited - Berlin 1930.

1934. Therapy of Lung Tuberculosis. Franz Deuticke, Wien - Leipzig 1934 (with monographies and X-ray pictures of the cases).

1954. Diet Therapy in Malignant Diseases (Cancer). Scala, Handbuch der Dietik, Wien, Franz Deuticke, 1954.

1958. A Cancer Therapy — Results of Fifty Cases. Totality Books.